ENGLAND
BEFORE
DOMESDAY

ENGLAND BEFORE DOMESDAY

Martin Jones

BARNES & NOBLE BOOKS
TOTOWA, NEW JERSEY

To Lucy

© Martin Jones 1986

First published 1986

First published in the USA 1986 by
Barnes & Noble Books
81 Adams Drive
Totowa, New Jersey, 07512

Library of Congress Cataloging-in-Publication Data

Jones, Martin, 1951–
  England before Domesday.

   1. Great Britain—History—To 1066. 2. England—
Antiquities. 3. Excavations (Archaeology)—England.
4. Environmental archaeology. I. Title.
   DA135.J66   1986   936.2   86-17405
ISBN 0-389-20668-7

Printed in Great Britain

Contents

Acknowledgements

I would first like to acknowledge the contribution of David Miles, whose own infectious enthusiasm for studies of the English landscape originally led to the idea of writing this book.

For reading and making valuable comments on sections of the text, I thank John Coles, Rosemary Cramp, Rob Foley, Anthony Harding, Colin Hazelgrove, Christopher Morris, Martin Millett, James Rackham, Lucy Walker and the series editor, Graham Webster. They are not to be held responsible for my idiosyncrasies and omissions.

The line drawings were executed at Durham University by Yvonne Brown, who I thank for adapting her archaeological draughting talents to a motley array of insects, wildcats, peat bogs and tree stumps with skill and sensitivity. For prompt and generous help with the acquisition of photographs, I thank Terry Betts, Graham Saxby Soafe and the Royal Commission on Historic Monuments, Arthur MacGregor and the Ashmolean Museum, John Coles and the Somerset Levels Project, Andrew Fleming and the Dartmoor Reeves Project, Anthony Harding, Tom Middlemas, Trevor Woods and the Department of Archaeology, Durham University.

Copyright for plates 1, 6, 7, 10, 12, 13, 19 and 20 rests with the Crown, for plates 2, 5 and 11 with the Ashmolean Museum, Oxford, and for plates 16 and 17 with the Somerset Levels Project.

Those who have unconsciously contributed to this book by the stimulating ideas they have offered in conversation are too numerous to cite in full, but I would like to mention Richard Bradley, Rob Foley, David Miles, Peter Reynolds and Lucy Walker.

Last but not least, I thank Michael Carrithers for his patient help with the production of the manuscript.

1

Back beyond history

In the winter of 1085, King William of England met with his council at Gloucester and engaged them in deep discussion. He subsequently sent his men all over England and into every shire to make a detailed survey of its manors and estates. The Anglo-Saxon Chronicle recalls the story:

> So very narrowly did he cause the survey to be made, that there was not a single hide nor a rood of land, nor was there an ox, or a cow, or a pig passed by, that was not set down in the accounts, and then all these writings were brought to him.

In compiling this survey, which later generations would call the Domesday Book, King William's commissioners left to posterity an astonishingly detailed account of the English landscape as they found it in the late eleventh century. It is an account that generations of scholars have pored over, and one that has made an enormous contribution to our understanding of how today's landscape came into being. In it we read of 'vills' whose names are easily identified with today's villages, and of the farmland and woodland that lay around them. Thanks to the work of W. G. Hoskins and others, we are able to trace the evolution of this Norman landscape through subsequent centuries, and to detect the legacies of previous landscapes that have survived, and which continue to determine the structure of today's landscape.

Yet the centuries since the compilation of the Domesday Book reflect no more than a final act in a very long environmental drama. The landscape it describes is already old in the sense that it has been tamed by its human occupants. Many parts of England are already filled with human settlement, and heavily given over to domestic plants and animals.

If we attempt to go back beyond the Domesday Book, to see how the landscape it describes came about, we are immediately faced with the paucity of written accounts. We can glean something from place names and from the charters that delineated Anglo-Saxon estates. We can also collect a few hints from early legislation about land holdings, but all of these take us back a further four centuries at the most. To get really far back, we must turn from the methods of history to those of archaeology.

Archaeology has a traditional image of being concerned with objects rather than landscapes, and sites rather than environments. It is not immediately obvious how a discipline whose main concern was once

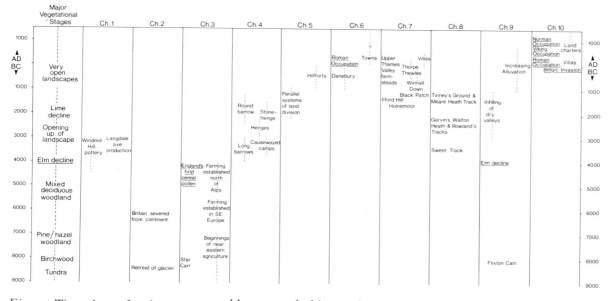

Figure 1 Time-chart of major environmental stages, alongside sites, events, and traditions cited in each chapter. The vertical axis is in calendar years, and the broken lines indicate extended durations within which the site/event etc. may be placed. Most of the prehistoric dates are calibrated radiocarbon dates, and therefore carry a potential margin of error often running to a few centuries.

pots and bones, and objects of metal and stone, might turn its attention to ancient farms and fields, and past woodlands and grasslands. Yet this is an area where archaeology has grown dramatically over the past few decades.

In the following pages, an attempt is made to draw on these new growth areas within archaeology, and to see what they can tell us about how the landscape described in King William's famous survey came into being. The different chapters will explore different episodes in the development of that landscape and the people that inhabited it. But before we can embark on this course, we must begin by looking at the methods that enable us to examine those distant episodes, and that is the topic of this first chapter. The methods concerned are those of *landscape archaeology* and *environmental archaeology*.

LANDSCAPE ARCHAEOLOGY

This branch of archaeology begins with the observation that there is a great deal more to be seen on the ground surface than just the ancient monuments known from guide books and Ordnance Survey maps. This is particularly true of ground broken by the plough. Most of our archaeological evidence lies just below the ground surface, where it is relatively well protected from the ravages of time that have honed away what evidence there once was above ground. Indeed the plough has been responsible for much of that honing, in the form of barrow-flattening, and settlement-levelling, and yet at the same time, by constantly bringing a sample of the buried evidence to the surface, it provides us with a valuable and retrievable record of past landscapes.

In this way, the plough may bite into a Roman rubbish pit and bring to the surface small pieces of tile-red pottery, Samian-ware, that was

Figure 2 Map of locations cited in Chapters 1–3.

brought to England from southern France 2000 years ago. A shower of rain may leave a flint flake the size of a thumbnail glistening in the furrow, chipped off to tip a hunter's arrow 6000 years earlier. Elsewhere along the ploughed surface other fragments may come into view: coarse earthenware fragments from prehistory, glazed wheel-turned pottery from the Middle Ages, a nineteenth-century ploughshare and a coin of George VI. The ploughed field is a scrambled record of all the human life that has passed across through the centuries. Those that passed may have added to the archive by living there, hunting there, or simply spreading out their household refuse with the farmyard manure.

Sometimes it may be difficult to tell what activity was involved, but occasionally the fragments on the surface may be quite explicit, as with metal-working slag, or the sharpening flakes from a stone axe. It may be that the patterning of the fragments on the surface provides a clue. They might, for instance, be dispersed thinly across the ancient fields to which they were added as fertiliser, or alternatively they may cluster densely within the rectangular outline of a building that once stood. In certain conditions we may even be able to discern a light discoloration along this outline, the fragmented stones and mortar that are all that remains of the building's walls. Elsewhere a localised concentration of pottery may fall within a patch of soil that is much darker than adjacent areas, the top of an old refuse pit, darkened by the ashes and organic waste thrown in with the broken pots.

The close and systematic scrutiny of all these features of ploughed fields, the patterning of fragmented objects, discoloured soil, and anything else that might provide a clue as to past human activity forms the basis of 'fieldwalking', a straightforward and crucial tool of landscape archaeology. Vast tracts of agricultural land in this country have in recent years been fieldwalked, and they have provided us with an extensive record of early landscapes. The other major tool of landscape archaeology takes place a few months later than fieldwalking, and, as well as a keen eye, requires a camera and a light aircraft.

Figure 3 The formation of cropmarks. Some subsoil features, such as wall foundations, depress crop growth, while ditches and pits filled with topsoil encourage it. The result is patterning in the growing crop.

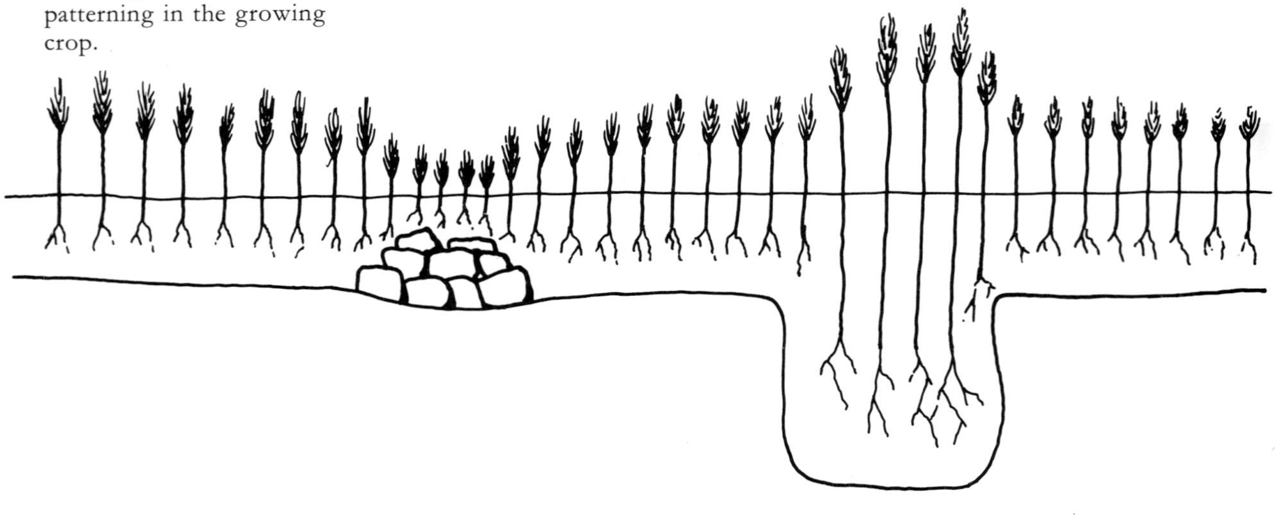

Archaeology from the air

Aerial photography also picks up features in ploughed land, but in this case during the growing season. As the crop is ripening, the stony soil along the line of the walls described above may bear stunted plants that ripen and change colour sooner than their neighbours. At the same time the deep organic soil of the nearby rubbish pit may support taller plants that stay green longer than the rest. In this way the patterns of artefacts and changing soil colour, that are seen in a freshly ploughed field, are replaced the following summer by patterns of variation in the colour and height of the growing crop.

To some extent the same thing may be observed in fields that are not ploughed, particularly after a dry summer has parched to a straw-brown colour all growth except for those plants growing above subsoil features, which they mark out as a green outline. These unploughed fields may also retain upstanding structures as well as something of the topography of earlier landscapes: the traces of a holloway, a slight field-bank, almost but not completely eroded by the ravages of time.

Plate 1 Cropmarks around Knowlton Henge, Dorset. The various regular circles are caused by the differential growth of crops over ditches and banks dug in prehistory and subsequently ploughed flat. It is the uneven subsoil that determines the pattern of crop growth (photo: J. Boyden).

These variations in the ground surface and the vegetation it supported make most sense when viewed or photographed from a few hundred metres up. The word 'photography' literally means 'drawing with light', and this describes perfectly its application to archaeology from the air. In different seasons and weather conditions, and at different times of day, the natural play of light and shadow on the ground will pick out these local fluctuations in various ways. A bank so slight as to be barely visible from the ground may throw a deep shadow when the sun is low in the sky; this will show up as a clear dark band on an aerial photograph.

The growth of aerial photography has revolutionised our understanding of early landscapes. Systematic flying has revealed enormous areas covered by ancient field systems and dotted with early

Plate 2 Aerial view of the early fields and lynchets on Fyfield Down (photo: Major G. Allen).

FYFIELD DOWN   3. 6. 34   4. 117.

settlements. In some areas these traces are so slight as to be invisible on the ground, and several aerial photographs are required to piece together its indistinct form. In other areas the traces are pronounced, and form striking images, both from the ground and from the air.

Fyfield Down: an ancient landscape

One such area lies to the north of Fyfield village near Marlborough in Wiltshire, not far from the impressive prehistoric monuments at Avebury and Silbury Hill. From a light aircraft flying northwards above Fyfield, the source of the massive sarsen stones that were dragged over the hills 4000 years ago to be erected at Avebury may be seen. They lie scattered in their natural location, the green riverless valleys that dissect these downs. From the air these small grey specks, which in fact weigh up to 60 tons each, might be mistaken for the flocks of sheep that have given sarsens their alternative name of 'grey-whethers'.

A short way further to the north, the grassy downs are peppered with patches of darker green, the crowns of clumps of woodland. In the open areas in between an impressive sight comes into view. Hundreds of hectares of downland are criss-crossed by earthworks, dividing what is open land today into 'fields' of all shapes and sizes. In places these fields fall into neat chequerboard patterns, elsewhere different land boundaries interleave and overlay one another, giving the crowded appearance of a railway junction.

On Fyfield Down, the boundaries of these defunct land divisions are sufficiently prominent to be seen from the ground as well as from the air (*Plate 2*). In some cases their boundaries are so prominent that moving from one field to the next involves a climb of 2–3m (7–10ft) up a steep slope. Such slopes are the faces of what are known as 'lynchets' – field-edge accumulations of soil that result from the field surface being loosened and rendered mobile by cultivation. The lynchets at Fyfield Down are so pronounced that they must, when they were still being cultivated, have had an appearance strangely reminiscent of the stepped hillslopes of South-East Asia.

While aerial photography may be able to conjure up these unfamiliar images, we generally rely on surface inspection and excavation to apply some date to them. In a ploughed area, fieldwalking may yield sufficient fragments of datable pottery or flint to ascribe a date. In the case of Fyfield Down, however, we must turn to excavation for a chronological framework.

An excavation was indeed undertaken in 1961, by Colin Bowen and Peter Fowler. A trench 15.5m (51ft) long by 1.8m (6ft) wide was laid out over one of the most prominent lynchets, and the soil that had built up to form the lynchet was peeled off, layer by layer, and all finds and structures recorded on the way. Beneath the soft dark turf, successive layers of chalky loam yielded some 90 small fragments of pottery. These, it was suggested, were introduced by muck-spreading over the years in which the field was being cultivated, and the chalky ploughsoil was moving downhill to form the lynchet. In the upper levels of the excavation, fragments of vessels were found that, although wheel-turned, lacked a glaze. They were recognised as being fragments of Roman pottery. Deeper within the lynchet, fragments of coarser hand-made pottery began to appear. These compare well with pottery known to date from the first and second millennia BC. A few hard and durable fragments coming from lugged pots could be ascribed to Windmill Hill pottery, found elsewhere on sites of the fourth millennium BC. If these fragments of pottery really were added to the fields by muck-spreading, then the fields truly are ancient. It would indicate that by the end of the Roman period, they had already been tended by over 100 generations of farmers.

An early landscape may thus be seen in plan and ascribed to a period of time, but we would wish to go much further than this bare outline. The shape of those fields does not tell us what crops grew within them, what animals grazed round about, and what birds flew overhead. A few pieces of broken pot say little of the lives of those who scattered them with the household refuse, in the hope of improving the subsequent harvest. Human landscapes are, by their very nature, organic, alive and ephemeral, and the search for the living elements takes us from landscape archaeology to environmental archaeology.

ENVIRONMENTAL ARCHAEOLOGY

The need to understand the living elements of a past landscape presents archaeologists with a major dilemma and challenge. The crops that grew in the field and the animals round about have long since been eaten or have decayed. The inert features may remain indefinitely within a landscape, but all life is bound to pass. That is the dilemma; the challenge is to find exceptions to this rule.

There are some rays of hope. A few fragments of the living landscape had indeed been conserved within the lynchet excavated at Fyfield Down. The fragments in question were not derived from any of the more visible features in the landscape, but instead from small animals sheltering within the ancient vegetation. While their soft tissues had been consumed by decay and predation, the shells of the land snails that lived among the fields had survived within the levels of eroded soil. Although the survival of such an unprominent component of the living landscape may seem to be of little significance to a study of that landscape from a human point of view, such evidence nonetheless contributed towards the reconstruction of those landscapes. These snail shells may be identified, in some cases to particular species known to favour particular habitat types.

Land snails are still common today on Fyfield Down and their ecology not surprisingly matches the short-turfed grassland that dominates the area. The relative abundance of the various species at the surface differs from what is found within the body of the lynchet. One species which is absent from the modern turf but present throughout the body of the lynchet is *Pomatias elegans*. This particular species of snail can be found

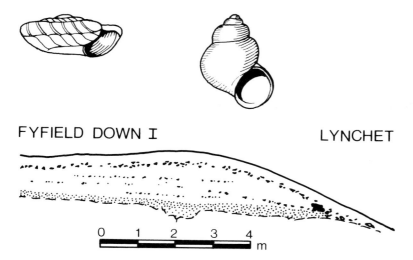

FYFIELD DOWN I   LYNCHET

Figure 4 A section through the Fyfield Down Lynchet (after J. G. Evans). Among the species of land snail recovered are *Discus rotundatus* (*above left*) and *Pomatias elegans* (*above right*). Scale refers to lynchet.

living on broken ground; it favours the loose soil into which it can easily burrow. The lack of such breaks in the modern turf would explain the absence of this species from the present surface, in contrast with the broken soil surface that must have prevailed during the formation of the lynchet.

At the very bottom of the lynchet a layer of soil was found that differed in appearance from the deposits found in the main body of the lynchet. It was believed to be a land-surface that preceded the formation of that lynchet. Within this soil, the relative abundance of the different species of snails was different again. The small, disc-shaped shells of *Discus rotundatus* were at their most frequent in this level. This is a common woodland species, occurring in leaf litter and under logs. It is one of a number of species in this lowest level with such a habitat preference, indicating that this early land surface was wooded.

These diminutive shells have thus added to our picture. The hint of broken ground comes as no surprise within such a field, but logs and leaf litter are another matter. There are indeed a few small copses within easy walking distance from the field, but not within easy crawling distance for a snail. A major change in the appearance of the landscape has to be entertained. This point is reinforced as one looks beyond Fyfield Down. Analyses of land snails have been carried out by John Evans on a number of sites in the limestone areas in which they flourish, and he has found a number of buried soils of early date in which woodland species predominate, even though the modern setting is open.

Such evidence from snails in this way provides some rather oblique indications of major changes in the living landscape. If only a little more had survived of such living landscapes, we could replace those oblique indications with much clearer images. Returning to the challenge this poses to archaeologists, dated deposits need to be found in which much more of the living landscape survives than a few empty snail shells. This means we must look for deposits in which the process of decay has been severely arrested, and we must now turn to consider where such deposits might be found.

Plate 3 Lake District: a view along Great Langdale (photo: author).

Deposits without decay

Decay is a biological process involving living organisms. Rotting tissue may be penetrated and engulfed by a mass of fungi, macerated by animals and further digested by bacteria. Like all other living things, these organisms are vulnerable to the loss of any of their basic requirements of life. In an arid soil they can die of 'thirst', and in a waterlogged soil they may 'drown'. They can also be poisoned by toxic salts within the soil. In order to capture evidence of living landscapes of the past, the archaeologist must actively seek out deposits in which the life of decay organisms is constrained in one of these ways. If England contained deserts, we might seek out deposits that lack water. As it is, we are better advised to seek out deposits that have a surfeit of water, to the exclusion of the air necessary for most forms of life.

Only the very wettest deposits are so free of air that decay is brought to a virtual standstill, but, once found, such sediments are a mine of information for the environmental archaeologist. To appreciate what potential lies in the examination of waterlogged deposits, we must move away from the well-drained downland around Fyfield in southern England, to the colder, wetter landscapes of the north.

Great Langdale: the potential of 'wet archaeology'

At a distance of 350km (217 miles) north of Fyfield Down lie the more rugged slopes of the Lake District. Here the rainfall is up to four times as great as it is at Fyfield Down, with parts receiving over 250cm (98in) a year. As on the Marlborough Downs, the Lake District has its share of prominent monuments to the human past. Stone circles and burial mounds interrupt many a treeless vista.

Even the bi-products of prehistoric activities may be found where they were discarded, as along the steep valley slopes of Great Langdale, north of Windermere, where waste-flakes and rough-outs of stone axes fashioned over 5000 years ago are to be seen, scattered among the hillside scree. Beyond these fragments from the human past, the present appearance of the area around Great Langdale gives a sensation of the forces of nature at work. Of the peak to the west of Langdale, Sca Fell, Wordsworth wrote:

> a temple built by God's own hand,
> mountains its walls, its gorgeous roof the sky

capturing the feeling of many who retreat from our towns to escape a while among the 'wilds' of the Lake District. It is indeed true that valleys such as Great Langdale (*Plate 3*) are fine examples of the immensely powerful forces with which nature has sculpted the landscape. The broad U-shape of the valley's profile bears witness to the glacier that tens of thousands of years ago demolished all protruding obstacles in its path. The haphazard scatter of hillocks at the head of the valley are the moraine, products of such demolition, unceremoniously dumped after a later advance of that multi-billion ton bulldozer. But in among these hillocks lie clues to another dimension to this landscape of which Wordsworth was not aware.

In contrast to these time-worn hillslopes, the valley floor towards the north is soft and spongy. This surface would take far less than a glacier to disturb and destroy it, and has clearly developed since the last glaciation in less violent epochs. Closer observation of this mossy mat into which the walker's boots gently sink reveals that it is still developing today.

Here we have found the waterlogged deposits for which we were searching, and in which we would hope that the exclusion of air has arrested decay. These boggy deposits are so important for environmental archaeology that it is worth pausing to consider how they are formed.

The growth of peat

The way in which they form does vary from place to place, but in the higher reaches of the valley at Great Langdale there is one plant that is particularly important in this process. This is a spongy light green moss whose Latin name is *Sphagnum*, and which is particularly common in the softer, soggier areas. With almost no effort it may be uprooted to reveal the lower parts of the plant. Apart from a change of colour, these are remarkably similar to the upper parts; beneath the green growing tops made up of spongy, spreading bracts, the stems have turned light brown but retained their form, and 10–20cm (4–8in) further down, the tissue darkens and becomes more limp. While dark and limp, these older stems are far from decayed. In this waterlogged environment, decay has been arrested and the *Sphagnum* is literally growing on top of itself. As growth proceeds, a backlog of undecayed organic debris accumulates, and it is this accumulation that is the young and spongy deposit forming parts of the valley floor at Great Langdale. This build-up is what we commonly call peat.

It is important to give an outline of how these peat deposits develop, as they provide a crucial part of the evidence for earlier landscapes. It is in these deposits that we may find fragments of the plants and animals that inhabited the contemporary landscapes around the successive layers of peat. By taking their ecological requirements into consideration, we may argue back from their presence to the form of the landscapes of which they were part.

Valley bottoms in a scoured glacial landscape are particularly conducive to the formation of peat, but they are not the only locations in which it is found. Nor is *Sphagnum* moss the only plant that will form into peat. Current conditions of soil and climate at the summits of our moorland areas also encourage the growth of the peat bogs. In general terms, the rugged glacial landscapes of the north and west of England, and in the low-lying fens such as in Somerset and East Anglia, provide a large number of deep peat deposits, and a smaller number have been found in southern England. Their detailed analysis has become a major tool in the understanding of early landscapes.

Such analysis may be conducted at various levels of sophistication, and some knowledge may even be gained from the most casual observation. Take, for example, a profile exposed by a rain gully dissecting the peat surface. Reaching down into the gully, an arm's depth might take you back years, centuries, or even millennia, according to how compressed the peat has become. If a handful of this darkened peat is picked apart, its fibrous texture is still recognisable as belonging to the stems and leaves of past vegetation.

A closer look within the gully might reveal a piece of prehistoric wood, or even a whole tree-stump, protruding from the exposed peat profile, its bark intact and unblemished. Such finds are striking, not only for the excitement of seeing and touching an organic part of a landscape that may be thousands of years old, but also because they may occur on a windswept moor that is today treeless. As with the snail shells from Fyfield Down, we can catch a glimpse of currently treeless landscapes in an earlier form, when they were still wooded, but within the peat we have more than a glimpse: we can see the actual trees.

This observation was originally made in the last century by a Scot named James Geikie. He recorded that Scottish peat bogs quite commonly contained layers of ancient tree-stumps, which he called 'forestian beds'. It was clear that there had been a whole series of episodes of landscape development since the glaciers left the land, and that during that development, areas which are now moorland had once been wooded.

The tree-stumps are but the tip of an iceberg. In our handful of peat, we may be able to pick out small hard seeds, to catch the iridescent gleam of an insect carapace, or disentangle a threadlike moss stem. With careful sampling and the aid of a microscope, we may identify even smaller objects. Indeed the most intensively studied component of peat bogs is also amongst the smallest, and that is pollen.

Pollen analysis at Langdale Combe

We can begin to see the importance of pollen to environmental archaeology by returning to the soft and spongy peat currently forming in Great Langdale, and considering what of today's landscape will be preserved in that peat.

At the head of the valley there is an old packhorse route that takes us up to Langdale Combe, where some of the deepest peat deposits in the valley are found. Here among the hummocks of moraine, such deposits have accumulated in the intervening hollows.

The surface of those hollows is dominated by the soft green crowns of *Sphagnum* moss, and these of course will form the major part of the accumulating peat deposit. In some places patches of heather have established themselves, and in others the white tufted heads of cotton grass decorate the bog surface. These plants will contribute leaves, stems, flowers and seeds to the growing peat. More of their tissue, together with the seeds and leaves of grasses, will be brought in by the braided streams scouring the steep hillslopes to either side. Seeds from berries may sporadically be introduced through bird droppings. In this way the seeds of such trees and shrubs as rowan, holly, juniper, yew and bilberry that cling to some distant rocky gully or sheltered crag may find their way into the growing bog.

All this would give us a general feeling of what the landscape was like, but if we had only these fragments from the bog, there is much that would escape our notice. We would probably remain oblivious to the patchwork of bracken and mat-grass covering much of the fells, and would find it impossible to gauge from the occasional bird dropping how much woodland was about. But as we look around the modern landscape we also remain oblivious to the invisible products of these plants with which the air is steeped. During spring and summer, billions of pollen grains and the spores of ferns and mosses travel from throughout the valley to settle on the surface of the bog. These pollen grains and spores will provide a much fuller picture of the landscape; a much wider range of plants will be detectable, and a broad estimate of relative abundance is possible.

If we again consider what of today's landscape will be preserved, but this time in the form of pollen and spores, a range of factors comes into play. We must bear in mind how much pollen, or how many spores, different plants are likely to release, and how far it is likely to travel. The 'pollen rain' at the head of the valley will again be dominated by the very local plants, the mosses, grasses and herbs growing among the hollows and hummocks, but the more distant hillslopes will also contribute a significant amount. As well as the bracken spores and grass pollen, the various trees and shrubs clinging to the crags and gullies will also release

Plate 4 Lake District: hummocks of glacial moraine towards the end of Great Langdale. The track visible on the right of the picture leads to Langdale Combe (photo: author).

pollen, in varying amounts according to species, to the wind. Much less of the pollen released outside the valley will reach the bog surface, but it will certainly be present. There may even be a trace of exotic pollen that has travelled thousands of kilometres.

The bog surface at Langdale Combe will in this way collect pollen and spores from both near and far afield. With an understanding of how pollen and spores are released from plants, and how they move about in the atmosphere, this microscopic collection can be sampled and deciphered to provide a detailed picture of the living parts of past landscapes. Such studies have been conducted in various parts of the Lake District including Langdale Combe itself. We can turn to a study conducted by Donald Walker at this site to see how 'pollen analysis' actually works.

The first stage of the analysis is the extraction in the simplest way possible of a vertical sequence of samples containing pollen and spores. At Langdale Combe, this was achieved by working a carefully constructed cylindrical device known as a Hiller borer into the bog surface. Each time the borer was pulled out of the peat, it contained within it a narrow cylinder of sediment of about 50cm (20in) in length. The borer would then be reinserted, and a further, deeper cylinder of sediment removed. In this way a full vertical sequence of samples could be taken back to the laboratory.

Progressive sampling in this way took the analysis down through 5m (16ft) of *Sphagnum*-rich peat corresponding to many centuries of accumulation in this small combe. The peat was found to be rich in the pollen of grasses, sedges and heather and, not surprisingly, the spores of *Sphagnum* moss. The tree and shrub pollen came largely from hazel, birch, alder, and oak, but juniper, holly and yew pollen were also found. Traces of beech pollen probably arrived by long-distance transport. The pollen and spores within the *Sphagnum* peat gave a general impression of a landscape not dissimilar to that of today.

The investigation did not stop there. A further 6m (20ft) of core below the *Sphagnum* peat were extracted before the coarse mineral sediments signalling glacial deposition were encountered. However, this lower section was not made up of *Sphagnum* peat. The bottom half of the 11m (36ft) studied was instead composed of layers of mud, which by their texture and composition could be seen to be the types of mud that form at the bottom of a lake. Indeed the fragments of bog-bean and

Figure 5 Pollen analysis at Langdale Combe. *Above left*: a section through the the deposits (adapted from D. Walker). *Below left*: schematic diagram of three of the pollen and spore types recovered (from left to right, oak, elm, and *Sphagnum* moss). *Right*: the Hiller borer used to extract the samples.

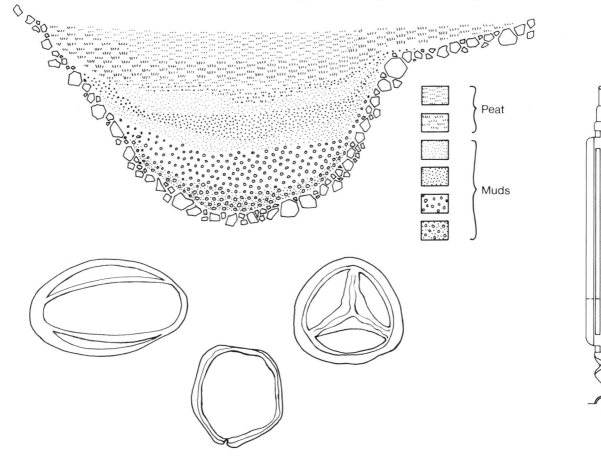

Peat

Muds

pond-weed lodged in these layers were reminiscent of the upland tarns or small lakes in which these plants still flourish. These pieces of evidence are clues to an earlier stage in the history of this hollow, when it was a lake or tarn, rather than a bog. Like peat, these lake sediments are ideal contexts for the study of pollen and spores, and alongside peat they form a major focus for pollen analysis.

The lake sediments below the peat at Langdale Combe varied in composition. The top 2m (7ft) were composed of coarse muds containing traces of sand, charcoal and humus, washed in from the surrounding landscape. These sediments were rich in the pollen of pondweed, and plants such as duckweed, meadowsweet, and the buttercup and daisy families peaked in the pollen record. We can easily imagine this small tarn in an open landscape, teaming with pondlife, the tangle of submerged stems and roots trapping the detritus that washed in from an unstable hillslope. The lower sediments tell quite a different story.

In contrast to the coarse detritus muds immediately below the *Sphagnum* peat, the bottom 3–4m (10–13ft) of the deposit were made up of the kinds of sediment that form beneath dark, but vegetatation-free water. The record of pollen and spores was markedly different from above. Five major components of the pollen and spore record of higher levels, heather, grasses, sedges, ferns and mosses, occurred as a mere trace. In addition, plantains and the buttercup family were gone from the record, and meadowsweet, scabious and the daisy family were found in far smaller numbers. The pollen and spores from these lower levels are dominated, not by low-growing moorland plants, but instead by large trees and shrubs. This surely corresponds to one of James Geikie's 'forestian beds' that left so many tree-stumps beneath the peat deposits of Britain. When these sediments were being laid down, we would have had to struggle up the valley and through branches and undergrowth to find our clear dark pool.

If we rebuild the whole sequence, the trees around this pool disappeared at a certain point. In the more open landscape that followed, the greater exposure to light encouraged the pond to fill with pondlife. At the same time the soils in the landscape around became sufficiently unstable to erode and collect in the pool. The conditions in the hollow gradually changed from open water to a bog. The boggy conditions provided a suitable environment for *Sphagnum* moss to grow, and this led in turn to the build-up of *Sphagnum* peat that we see today.

The Elm Decline

Just as tree-stumps are widespread in peat deposits, so are the many details of the pattern described above widespread in pollen sequences. At many sites, including Langdale Combe, the transition from wooded to open conditions is accompanied by a drop in the pollen of elm, and the appearance of pollen of such herbs as mugwort and plantain. These herbs are characteristic of open, disturbed ground. Disturbance of the landscape is also reflected in the traces of eroded sand and humus that were noticed at the same levels within Langdale Combe that contained these herbs.

Disturbance by fire is also evident as fragments of charcoal, encountered at a depth of 6m (20ft) within the deposits. Such hints of clearance, fire, and soil disturbance may be compared with evidence from the nearby pollen-site of Barfield Tarn, which lies to the south-west of Great Langdale, towards the Cumbrian coast. Here, the rise in herbs is accompanied by a dramatic inwash of the boulder clay that had lain upon the steep slopes around the tarn.

Among the pollen types appearing at this time, here and elsewhere along the Cumbrian coast, are the pollen grains of cultivated cereals. These indications of fire, clearance, soil disturbance, and cultivation lead us to ask what the human population was doing at this time. With the technique of calibrated radiocarbon dating, this transition between woodland and open ground can be placed around the end of the fifth millennium BC, a period that had seen the emergence of farming in this country. It is during this same period that fragments of Windmill Hill pottery were scattered by early farmers over Fyfield Down.

One of the durable artefacts of the period is the polished stone axe, such as was produced in quantity along the hillslopes of Great Langdale. The stone from which these axes were made is sufficiently characteristic for axes found elsewhere in the country to be attributed to this source. One such axe has been found within peat deposits at Barfield Tarn. Others have been found as far afield as the south coast of Britain. We can therefore envisage a farming community in the late fifth/early fourth millennium BC existing within an extensive network of contacts, and which we expect could exert considerable influence over the surrounding landscape by means of cutting down trees, burning vegetation, grazing animals and cultivating the soil.

When plantain spread rapidly across New England, the American Indians gave it the name 'white man's foot', illustrating its close relationship with the new settlers. We can surely see a parallel with the similar spread of a species of plantain across 'old' England, 6000 years earlier. That early episode of landscape development, when the woodlands began to open up, must have owed a great deal, if not all, to the activities of early farming communities.

Wordsworth would undoubtedly have been surprised to learn how much the development of the Lake District landscape had been diverted by human action. Poets and travellers have often sought reassurance in the sense of timelessness that England's remoter regions instil. Yet the illusory nature of the Lake District's wild appearance is by no means unique. Techniques such as pollen analysis have now shown repeatedly that a wide range of 'wild' and rural landscapes bear the deep imprint of the forces of past human endeavour, and the present form of central and remote regions of England alike are the culmination of several millennia of such forces. During these millennia, landscapes have been reorganised, vegetation has been cleared, and soils have been heavily worked. In intervening episodes, when these forces have been relaxed, the landscape has reverted as aggressively to a different, primeval form in which the human species is but one member of a diverse and sometimes hostile ecosystem.

Fyfield Down and Great Langdale provide examples of how it is possible for archaeology to take the study of the landscape back beyond the Domesday Book, but these two examples only scratch the surface. The forms of evidence available to us are as diverse as the ecosystems that are being explored. Both environmental and landscape archaeology continue to develop new ways of tackling new kinds of data. In the following pages we focus in more closely on the past landscapes they allow us to discern.

2

Searching for a wildscape

The story must begin somewhere, and, since we are dealing with human landscapes, let us start at a time when the land was truly wild, and the human imprint not yet visible. This means, of course, going back beyond the changes outlined in the previous chapter, beyond the attack mounted by early farmers upon their wooded environment.

The pollen record suggests that the impact of these early farmers was considerable. Yet it also indicates that the preceding millennia were by no means free from change. There is no permanent and unchanging pollen assemblage that characterises the pre-agricultural levels of peat bogs and lake sediments. If we look in detail at the lower sediments in Langdale Combe they do not stabilise at a fixed set of trees and shrubs in particular proportions, but continue to change in content and proportion. They are changing still as the Hiller borer reaches the angular mineral particles of the moraine itself, and the deposition of moraine marks the massive changes that accompanied the heaving and thrusting of ice sheets during the last glaciation.

THE ICE AGE

In other words, if we look for a permanent and unchanging landscape, then we are searching in vain. If we switch for a moment from an archaeological timescale to a geological timescale, and think in terms not of thousands but of millions of years, then we can see this constant change in context. We live in a geological period which is known as the Quaternary Epoch, which has so far lasted for around two million years. Using methods similar to those described in the previous chapter, but applied to sediments deposited in the more distant past, geologists have shown that this epoch has been characterised by massive climatic change. The earth's temperature has fluctuated to such an extent that on repeated occasions, and for extended periods, massive snowfalls have failed to melt and have instead coalesced into enormous ice-sheets, or glaciers. Then in intervening periods, the warmer temperatures have liberated the vast quantities of water in those glaciers, returning them to the sea. This cyclical process is what has given the Quaternary Epoch its more familiar name, the Ice Age.

It is during these alternating periods of global freezing and thawing that our own species, *Homo sapiens*, has evolved and become so successful on the planet. Since the 'hominids' from which we evolved first colonised Europe almost a million years ago, ice-sheets have advanced, and then retreated, from substantial parts of its land surface on at least eight occasions.

In searching for a 'wildscape', it is clear therefore that we should not be looking for a fixed and timeless natural setting into which the human species or its immediate forerunners introduced change. That would bear no relation to reality. The wildscape should instead be likened to a moving horse onto which humans have jumped. The horse has its own momentum, with or without the rider, but with time the rider may change the horse's pace, and even the direction in which it travels.

In view of the dynamic nature of this system, our account could begin at various places. It could start with the first evidence of humans or our hominid forerunners on the land surface that is now England, in the form of chipped stone deposited a quarter to a half a million years ago.

We cannot rule out the possibility that the tiny populations that occasionally migrated to this remote corner of the Old World may have modified their landscape, but the evidence is slight. The pollen record from previous interglacials does occasionally suggest the existence of woodland clearings, and small fragments of charcoal the occurrence of fire. Whether we can put these together and associate them with our ancestors is open to debate. Such archaeological evidence as they have left behind has been exposed to the ravages of subsequent glaciations. All but the most durable artefacts, their stone tools, had a minimal chance of survival.

We can gain a clearer impression of what has happened since the most recent of these destructive glaciations. It is in the current interglacial, known as the Flandrian, or more optimistically, the 'post-glacial' period, that our own species has reached very large numbers, and they have left a far more substantial body of data than their predecessors. It will (we hope) be several thousand years before a future glacial advance erases this record. In the meantime I have chosen to begin this account with the beginning of the Flandrian period.

AFTER THE LAST GLACIATION

The most recent retreat of the glaciers began just over 10,000 years ago. The ice-front withdrew to the north leaving a land-surface still governed by the harsh conditions of permafrost, and now scoured by the massive erosive powers of the rapid release of millions of gallons of water from melting glaciers. As summers gradually became warmer, grasses and ferns and various hardy heathland shrubs such as crowberry made use of the short growing season in areas that escaped the heaviest erosion. We can imagine a landscape in many ways similar to modern Lapland, with a lichen-speckled heath stretching out for miles, punctuated by a mosaic of sedges and grassy swards around seasonal lakes and bogs.

Under the overcast winter sky, the tundra would be at its most bleak. Under the summer sun, the lakes and pools would attract migratory birds in vast numbers, and herds of reindeer and wild horse would collect around the water's edge. We can imagine them looking up from the water, their nimble limbs tensing, and the birds around them noisily taking to the air as danger is sensed, perhaps in the form of a wolf, or a human.

We can explore these landscapes and their occupants, not only by looking at the pollen record, but also by studying the remains of large and small animals within archaeological deposits. We might find a fragmented reindeer bone bearing the tooth-marks of a wolf, or the axe-marks of a human. We might also recover fragments of the smaller animals that roamed the tundra – hares, shrews, even spiders and insects. They too enrich our perception of these early landscapes.

The speed with which insects can colonise new habitats makes them excellent indicators of the precise rate of climatic change. The early appearance of warmth-loving species reflects the speedy amelioration of the Flandrian climate. Conditions were soon warm enough for the fruits of larger woody plants, carried from the south by wind and birds, to germinate and grow.

The low mats of crowberry that dominated the early heath were soon peppered with the light green foliage of birch and the darker coloured juniper. Both occurred as dwarf forms, carrying their stems within inches of the ground. It was not only the short growing season that kept taller plants at bay; it was also the searing periglacial winds that tore across these vast open spaces, threatening any upstanding plant with their violent dust-storms. The dust deposited by these winds can still be seen; they form some of the 'brickearths' of the south-east.

The development of a wooded landscape

It was only as the temperature gradients softened and these winds settled that the spindly trunks of silver birch could replace the dwarf form to reach 3m or 4m (10ft or 13ft) into the sky. A few centuries after the last glacial retreat, such birchwoods had sprung up throughout the country.

Some impression of the appearance of these early birchwoods may be gained from looking at parts of modern Iceland or Lapland. The shelter of these modestly-sized birch trees would have harboured a more luxurient vegetation than the preceding windswept heath. The migrating herds of the tundra would be less well adapted to the closed environment of the birchwood than smaller groups of red deer, elks, and wild cow or 'aurochs'. As the climate became more gentle, trees would get bigger. As time went on the various large mammal populations would have to come to terms with darker, more closed environments.

As the growing season became long enough for more lofty trees to establish, the birch woodland would reach 15–20m (49–66ft) in height. The stands of old contorted trunks that line the valleys of Caithness in Scotland give an impression of these more developed birchwoods. The abundance of fallen, lichen-encrusted trees, rotting on the mossy forest floor, is very typical of unmanaged woodlands. These older trees would be removed from today's rather tidy woodlands, which differ markedly in appearance from the matted form of virgin woodland, where death and decay have as much a place as life and growth.

In these changes in the form of birchwoods through time, from dwarf birch through 4m (13ft) to 20m (66ft) stands, we see a pattern that will continue as the climate grows warmer and the growing season longer. The length and quality of this season sets a limit on the quantity of living matter a given area of soil can support. It is generally true that ecosystems which are not restricted by other factors such as drought or over-exploitation, tend to approach that 'climatic' limit. Thus the polar regions support a thin layer of tundra heath, in contrast to the enormous depth of rain forest found in the tropics. On a smaller scale, the gradual warming of the climate and lengthening of the growing season that followed the retreat of the glaciers from the English land mass, slowly raised the limit on 'ecological productivity' and gradually allowed a deeper and denser woodland cover to form.

This trend had critical consequences for the birch woodland. Birch trees are fast and efficient colonisers of open ground, but there are limits to the depth and density of the woodland they can form. They have a short life span of around 50 years, and during this time are unlikely to exceed 20m (66ft) in height. The old encrusted trunks found in the Scottish highlands probably mark the limits of growth for birch. Were they not kept in check by muir-burning and grazing it seems likely that the taller stems of Scots pine would invade these woods. Once established, the dense pine canopy would shield the sun's rays from the lower leaves of the birch trees, and they would succumb in that major battle of woodland ecosystems, the competition for light.

This is certainly what began to happen in many parts of England within a millennium of the last glacial retreat. As the limits of productivity increased, birch woodlands were replaced by a plant community with a greater potential productivity. The fresh green birch foliage that blanketed the land surface was gradually overshadowed by dark green pine needles.

The ancient pinewoods

The pinewoods of modern England give us little clue as to the appearance of the wild pinewoods of prehistory. The regimented rows of identical trunks that form the even, solid canopy of modern woods are a human artifice. Conifers today are cultivated in much the same way as a cereal crop, and subjected to similar chemical and genetic control. There is much more genetic variation in a wildwood, and prehistoric pinewoods would have taken a far more varied and changeable form. Just as humans come in various shapes and colours, so do plants and animals that have not been subjected to artificial breeding and selection. In the ancient forests of Rothiemurchus in Perthshire, and Ballochbuie in Aberdeen, we can still see this variation among the wild Scots pines. Some start life in a conical, Christmas-tree-like form, which gradually develops into a rounded, elm-like crown. There are also dome-shaped, columnar and flat-topped trees in these woods.

Another tree which, judging from the pollen evidence, was abundant in these early pinewoods was hazel. Like the pine trees, the hazels would also have adopted a form which was quite different from their modern counterparts.

The hazel most commonly seen in today's landscape is found in small patches of woodland scattered around rural settlements. They are remnants of woods that have been managed and cut by generations of woodmen, and in the process have acquired a characteristic shrubby form, each clump made up of several springy poles rather than a single trunk. The hazel trees that flourished in the early pinewoods would not have been of this form. We must envisage instead far more lofty trunks than most modern hazels bear, reaching the woodland canopy alongside the pines.

The methods of woodland management that have prevented modern hazels from adopting this form have gone into marked decline during this century. As a result, many of our surviving hazels are straggly and overgrown. It may be that future generations will see these trees revert to the loftier forms they adopted in the early pinewoods, provided of course that any small woods survive in our countryside.

So when piecing together the evidence of peaks in the pine and hazel pollen of this era, we must entertain a range of forms of woodland quite different from those we see today. The varied mosaic of Scots pine and hazel trees of all shapes and sizes would share as much in common with a modern conifer plantation as a pack of wolves with a French poodle. As well as being varied it would be changing, in pace with the continuing changes in the climate. The undergrowth nestling between trunks of hazel and pine would quite literally harbour the seeds of such change, in the form of acorns, and the nutlets of elm and lime.

These seeds would have been brought in by large birds and small mammals, and in the case of lime, been carried along by wind and water. They would at first have germinated to form glades of moderately-sized trees, enjoying the shelter of the loftier woodland that continued to dominate the landscape. These deciduous trees had, however, the potential to form a richer and deeper woodland than the pine/hazel woodland in which they at first found shelter. A further improvement of the climate would allow their broad leaves to mop up more of the sunlight and support these richer ecosystems. In many parts of the country by 6000 BC, the dark green crowns of pine were struggling to compete for light with the rich green foliage of oak, lime and elm.

Broadleaf woodlands
Like the pine trees they overtook, these new species would also have a different appearance from their modern counterparts. Indeed, the word 'appearance' implies a suitable vantage point, something far more accessible to us as we stand back to admire the majestic oaks of modern parkland, than to the humans that clambered amidst the dense undergrowth of a wildwood. By the sixth millennium BC, the woodland would in many places have closed up to form a cathedral of long straight

trunks disappearing into a dense high canopy, and the 'appearance' of woodlands such as these would have been the appearance of their dark interiors.

The ground surface would have assumed a quite different aspect now that the major quest for light was taking place at a greater height. The plants found would be those that could grow quickly and flower before the deciduous leaves had blotted out the sun, such as bluebells and wood anemones. The wild cattle and deer would be scattered more thinly, now that low-growing browse was less available. The most accessible food source would lie below the scatter of rotting trunks within the leaf litter. The fruits, seeds, leaves and small invertebrates would be sought out by hedgehogs, shrews, woodmice, bank voles and wild boars.

Looking up from the forest floor, a great deal of variety would be seen among the tall straight trunks. Some would be healthy and firm, bearing a dense head of foliage. Others would be past their best, and shafts of light would be falling through their sparser crowns. Within the intensely competitive woodland ecosystem, a flush of ivy would grab this opportunity to borrow the trunk and reach the distant canopy, throttling its host in the process. An even older tree, no longer producing leaves, and having become a passive ladder for the smothering ivy, would come crashing to the ground, riddled with fungi and insects. As it hit the forest floor, hoards of stag- and deathwatch-beetles would come scurrying from the leaf litter and other decaying trunks to continue the demolition.

In the process, a small clearing will have been created, and a rather different sequence of events will ensue. For a season or two, the normally restricted ground-living herbs will enjoy a bonanza of light. A strong wind might bring in a few birch seeds which are now able to establish themselves in this opening. Wild cattle and deer will naturally seek out such openings for their rich browse, and continue their visits as the birch is overtaken by hazel. The hazel will in turn give way to the larger deciduous trees and the canopy will once again close up.

ECOLOGICAL SUCCESSION

This sequence, lasting a generation or two, will have mirrored the sequence experienced by the whole woodland over the previous 3000 years. This is quite a typical ecological process known as succession. The general principal is that as an ecosystem progresses towards the limits of productivity for the area it occupies, it does so in a specific sequence of steps, each one characterised by a form of vegetation with a greater productive capacity than its predecessor. Thus if we compare an open land surface created as a continent is exposed beneath a retreating glacier, with one created within a woodland by a falling tree, then the difference in scale is enormous, but the ecological succession is surprisingly similar.

The process of ecological succession can also be approached from a geographical standpoint. If we look for the glaciers today, we find that they have retreated as far north as the northern parts of Scandinavia. Around the glaciers is a belt of tundra, merging into birch woodland, such as can be found in the northern parts of Scotland. These in turn give way to pinewoods, and further south to broadleaved woodlands. In a simplified schematic form the glaciers are at the core of a series of concentric bands of vegetation, reflecting stages in the ecological succession described above. As these successive bands reach further south, into more climatically favourable areas, so is the vegetation within them able to reach greater levels of ecological productivity.

Ebb and flow

We can add the element of time to this model of bands of vegetation across Europe, in order to gain further insight into the ecological workings of the Quaternary Epoch. As the temperature has fluctuated during this two million year period, so have the glaciers advanced to the south, and then retreated to the north. In view of the link between temperature and productivity, the concentric bands of vegetation would be expected to slowly ebb and flow in sequence with the movement of the glaciers. At any one point in the landscape, these tides will wash backwards and forwards with each fluctuation. As the temperature shifted from a cold extreme to a warm extreme, so would a glacial retreat be followed at that point in the landscape by a birch stage, a pine stage, and eventually a broadleaf stage. As the temperature returned to a subsequent cold extreme, then an ebb in these tides would become a flow. The broadleaf stage would be replaced by pine, birch and tundra stages in sequence, and tundra would be smothered by the advancing glacier.

Mountains and coastlines

Having outlined a general model of ebb and flow of vegetational zones to explain the dynamics of the Quaternary Epoch, we must adjust it to account for the fine detail of the English land surface. We have been treating the European continent as if it were some vast homogenous plain over which bands of vegetation have freely moved back and forth, but of course it is not. It has mountains and it has coastlines, and each of these will affect the way in which the various vegetational zones ebb and flow in response to climatic change.

In terms of the north European climate, there are some similarities between ascending a mountain and travelling northwards on level ground. In each case the temperature drops and the growing season diminishes. It is hardly surprising that there is also a similarity in the banding of vegetation. As one proceeds northwards through Europe and Scandinavia at a particular altitude, broadleaf, pine, birch, and tundra belts are encountered in turn. Precisely the same sequence is encountered when gaining altitude on a European mountain. Thus, long after the tundra belt has left the English lowlands, crowberry heath still lingers on at high altitudes, and below this heath are belts of birch, and then pine.

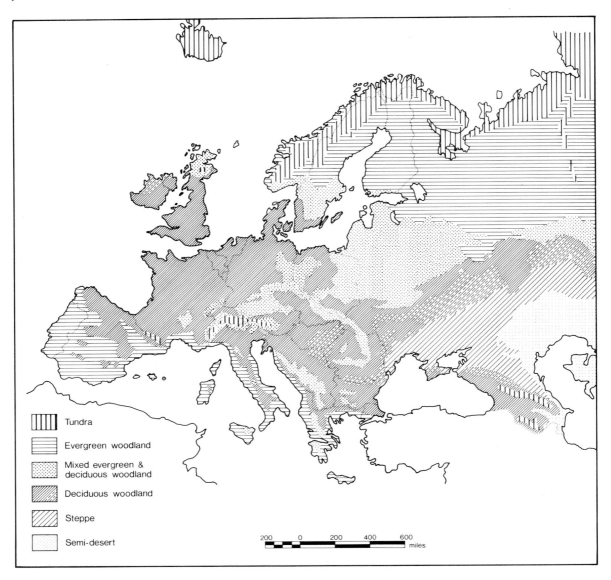

Figure 6 The hypothetical
climax vegetation of Europe.
(adapted from S. R. Eyre
1963 *Vegetation and soils*).

Legend:
- Tundra
- Evergreen woodland
- Mixed evergreen & deciduous woodland
- Deciduous woodland
- Steppe
- Semi-desert

This parallel can be extended to change through time. In a subsequent glacial advance, when open tundra spreads again in advance of the glaciers, that mountain heath and those belts of birch and pine will also move downhill. This can be seen in the pollen record. Just as the pollen evidence from low-lying bogs and lakes chronicles the ecological ebb and flow in latitude, so does the pollen evidence from upland lakes provide evidence of a concurrent ebb and flow in altitude.

The coastlines introduce yet another dimension to the story. The position of Britain's coast has shifted considerably since the retreat of the glaciers, and this is largely due to the enormous quantities of water involved in the freezing and thawing of glaciers. During the coldest

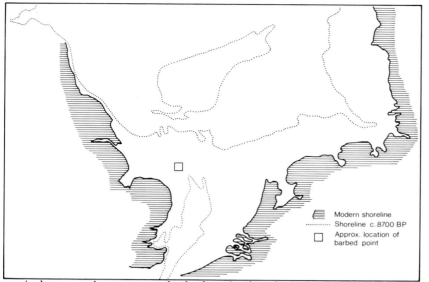

Figure 7 Changes in the North Sea shoreline in the Flandrian period, showing the area from which the worked antler tip to an early hunter's spear or harpoon was dredged up (adapted from H. Godwin 1975 *History of the British Flora*, and E. Oele *et al.* 1979 *The Quaternary history of the North Sea*).

period, so much water was locked up in the glaciers overlying Europe that the shallower seas, such as the North Sea, ran dry, and the land surfaces of Britain and Europe were part of a single continuum. As the glaciers melted, the seas swelled and once again spread into the British Channel and the North Sea. The final land link was severed around 8500 years ago. By the time broadleaf woodland had engulfed the English land surface, Britain was once more an island. Any further spread of vegetation from the south was now impeded by a continuous barrier of seawater.

Fragments of the landscape flooded in this process are occasionally dredged up by trawlers working in the North Sea. These pieces of 'moorlog' can be treated in much the same way as the peat fragments discussed in the last chapter. They may contain a tree-stump from the vast tracts of prehistoric woodland submerged by the sea. They will certainly contain the pollen that allows us to place those woodlands within the vegetation sequence outlined in this chapter. We might even retrieve some trace in these moorlog fragments of the humans that roamed the North Sea bed when it was still dry land.

One such piece of evidence was dredged up in 1932 from the Leman and Ower banks, some 50km (31 miles) from the modern Norfolk coast. The fishermen recovered within their catch a barbed point fashioned from a sliver of antler. Such implements were used to tip the spears and harpoons wielded by hunting bands in the early Flandrian period.

As well as burying vast areas of land, the expanding sea created a whole new series of coastal environments. The world's coastal zones have yielded some of its most productive ecosystems, and they have consequently formed a prominent part of the human landscape. However, the areas that made up England's coastal zone during the progressive severance of Britain's land-bridge with Europe have themselves been lost under subsequent advances of the sea.

As well as obscuring the coastline around some parts of Britain, the flooding of the North Sea exposed stretches of coast in other parts. The sheer weight of water and sediment coming into the North Sea tilted the British land-mass such that contemporary coastlines in parts of Scotland were raised up rather than submerged. By looking at these ancient raised beaches we can gain some impression of the coastal environment around the wildwood.

At various points along these raised coasts in Scotland, the debris left by its human inhabitants still survives as organic 'midden' deposits, frequently buried within sand dunes. The debris of meat consumption amassed in these middens allows us to construct a picture of the rich diversity of animal life that had developed around the coast, by the time the climatic amelioration levelled off around 8500 years ago.

Looking out from the northern shores we might have seen seals, rorquals and dolphins. Guillemots would be flying up above, along with the great northern diver, and a bird which failed to survive into the twentieth century, the great auk. The tidal zone would be rich with molluscs and crabs, and several types of fish would swim in the coastal waters.

Looking back towards the land, the lofty wildwood would dominate the skyline. The wind, salt spray and instability of the ground surface could well have constrained this vegetation from reaching the shore. The wildwood might instead have given way to a rugged scrubby mat of sea buckthorn, its contorted stems reaching little more than shoulder height. This scrubland might in turn fragment into open spaces that lead down to treeless mudflats and beaches of shingle and sand.

Just as the coastal zone would add an element of variety to the intransigent progress of wildwood succession, so would the land-water interfaces of the interior. The inland lakes and rivers, many of them having newly carved out their beds since the devastation of the most recent glaciation, would have been greatly affected by the global changes described in this chapter. Not only would there have been enormous fluctuations in the volumes of water collecting within them, but they would be recovering ecologically from glacial devastation in the same way as the neighbouring ecosystems on dry land. The birds would return quickly, and the reed-beds that colonised the swampy margins of larger lakes would have harboured crane, white stork, ducks, grebes, mergansers and lapwings. Salmons and eels would soon be seasonally migrating upstream, but other familiar fish, such as perch and pike, may have taken some time to recolonise all of England's rivers.

Where the banks were more stable, the fully developed wildwood would have come right down to and overhung the water's edge. Indeed the broader rivers would have provided one of the best views of the wildwood from the outside. A journey would have been Amazonian in flavour, the dense foliage banking up on either side. Such journeys would have revealed the broadleaved wildwood of 8000 years ago in its full richness and diversity.

The rivers of the north, such as the Tyne, the Tees and the Ouse, would have taken us past sloping banks thick with oak and hazel. In their upper reaches we might still find remnants of more ancient woodland cover, such as the juniper woods that may still be seen in Upper Teesdale. To the south of the country, rivers such as the Thames and the Great Ouse would have been filled with the delicate scent of the limewoods whose pale bluish-green foliage would rise up behind the dark green alder carrs. In the south-west, the Exe and the Tamar would take us through stands of wych elm.

The sounds would be of birdsong, and a wide variety of woodland birds would be heard, perhaps alongside the trumpeting of some distant crane by the water's edge. A roe deer might be silently moving along the banks, where the foliage was within reach. Just as the various plants fit in to an overall ecological pattern, so do these animals, and to see how, we must turn to another model, the 'ecological pyramid'.

Predators, prey, pyramids and chains

Let us consider the roe deer in more detail. Today this animal feeds largely off the foliage of broadleaved trees, especially hazel. In spring, before the leaves are fully out, it will eat the young buds or the spring herbs that flourish in the seasonally open canopy. During winter it is able to adapt to a drastic reduction in food intake.

Because of these eating habits, the roe deer is well adapted to life in a deciduous woodland. The elk presents a different story. This species prefers the rich undergrowth of an open marshy woodland to the dark decaying floor-cover beneath a dense stand of broadleaved trees. In wintertime it can make do with eating birch and pine bark, but may go hungry in woods composed of other species. The elk is clearly well adapted to birch woods and the more open of the pine/hazel woods.

It follows that, as the birch, pine, and broadleaf belts have moved back and forth during the Quaternary Epoch, so have the populations of roe deer and elks moved with the particular vegetation belts to which they are best suited.

Different animals vary in how flexible they are about environment and food source. Red deer are far more versatile in their habitat range than either roe deer or elks, and they may move among a variety of habitats within a single lifetime. In present day Scandinavia, reindeer too make use of different zones at different times, moving from the birchwoods in spring to the open tundra in summer.

At the other extreme, some animals are tied to one specific foodstuff, and must stay firmly within a particular vegetation zone. One such example is a woodland beetle by the name of *Ernoperus caucasicus*. Fragments of this small animal have been recovered from the peaty remnants of England's prehistoric wildwood, and today the living animal can be found beneath the bark of lime trees, on which it exclusively feeds. During the ebbing and flowing of the vegetation zones, this beetle would, needless to say, have stayed firmly within that part of the broadleaf belt that was rich in lime trees.

These close relationships between particular species and their food

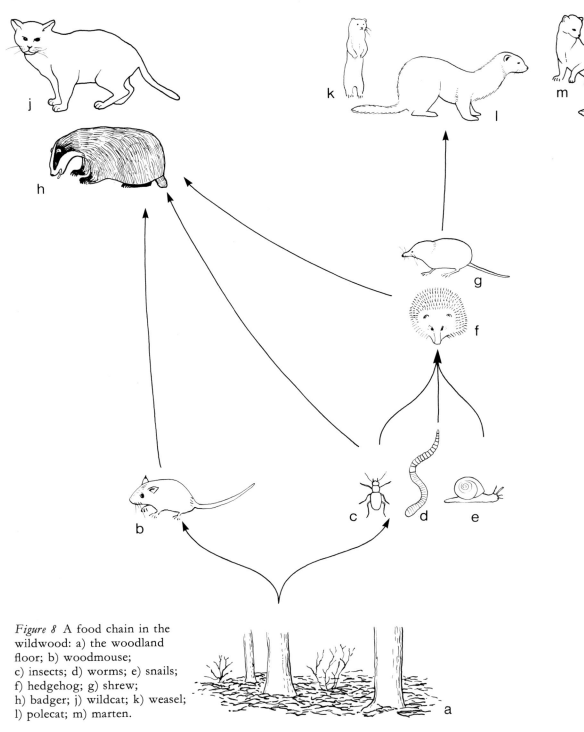

Figure 8 A food chain in the wildwood: a) the woodland floor; b) woodmouse; c) insects; d) worms; e) snails; f) hedgehog; g) shrew; h) badger; j) wildcat; k) weasel; l) polecat; m) marten.

sources are subject to a delicate balancing mechanism. It is well known that woodland deer are quite able to debark and destroy the trees that form their habitat. We also know that another species of bark beetle has recently, by spreading Dutch elm disease, decimated our elm populations.

In the wild, such destructive processes are as dangerous for the predator as for the prey. By destroying their habitat and source, animals create their own wilderness and perish in turn. As a result, the animal populations that are most successful in the long term are those that stabilise at numbers their food sources can accommodate. Should they for some reason exceed those numbers, they will begin to destroy their food source, which will then become scarce. As food becomes scarce, less animals will survive. With less animals around, the food source is able to grow back to its original abundance. With the food source once again abundant, the animals can multiply, and the whole process starts again.

In other words, the system stabilises itself, and it does so in a way that leads to the formation of an ecological pyramid. To take the example of the leaf litter below a wildwood; at the base of the pyramid is a large quantity of vegetable matter. At the level above are the animals that feed upon it – beetles and other insects, worms, snails and a wide range of invertebrates. These in turn are the food source of another series of animals – shrews, voles, hedgehogs and woodmice – which occupy the next level in the pyramid. Also stalking the wooded areas are animals that occupy an even higher level – the weasels, polecats and martens that prey upon these small woodland mammals.

As has been described above, each level will tend towards equilibrium with the level below, such that populations remain sufficiently small, so as not to over-consume their own food source. We can take this process one step further, by taking into consideration the system's inherent inefficiency.

When shrews eat insects, or weasels eat shrews, only a small proportion of the calories in their diet is turned into fresh body tissue. By far the larger part of those calories is dissipated as heat. Shrews and weasels are not unusual in this respect, such inefficiency is the norm within ecological pyramids. As a result, the sheer bulk of living matter decreases rapidly as one moves up the pyramid. So, weight for weight, the occupants of each successive level will occur in progressively smaller quantities, and most sequences will peter out at around the fourth or fifth level. We can now see why this sequence is described as an ecological 'pyramid'.

If we return to the gradually shifting vegetation zones, then each of these will carry its own ecological pyramid of plants, animals, fungi and micro-organisms. We could, for example, contrast the wildwood pyramid described above with an open tundra pyramid occupying the English land surface soon after the last glaciation.

Feeding on the lichen-encrusted crowberry heath would be a range of invertebrates, various birds including red grouse and capercailzie, and such mammals as mountain hare and reindeer. The next level of the pyramid would be split into various sectors. The invertebrates would be taken by pigmy shrews, which themselves would be taken along with the birds and hares by foxes, stoats and birds of prey. The larger mammals would be consumed by wolves, bears and humans.

This picture is complicated by the versatility of many of the animals within these various pyramids. Mention has already been made of how red deer can migrate from one zone to another, varying its food source as it goes. Foxes are another highly adaptable feeder. The effect of these various versatile species is to introduce cross-links within and between the various pyramids, knitting them together into what is often described as a 'food web'.

Our total ecological model for the Quaternary Epoch is thus a series of vegetation zones, modified by landforms and coastlines, fluctuating back and forth along with changes in global temperature, advancing and retreating both in latitude and altitude. Superimposed on this is a complex food web that links all organisms into various ecological pyramids, each equilibrating with particular vegetation zones, whose fluctuations they follow.

Humans within the ecosystem

We can now turn to see how humans fit into this complex and dynamic structure. The best and most durable evidence we have of what early humans ate is in the form of meat bones, and it is through this part of their diet that we can slot them into the food web. Prominent among the debris from the caves and camps occupied by humans during the last full glaciation in north-west Europe are the butchered bones of reindeer. We can also find their antlers, elegantly worked into harpoon heads for further hunting.

In addition, those distant hunters have left a remarkable record of their activities in the cave art of Spain and France. Many a hunting scene survives in these designs, showing not just reindeer, but also red deer, horse, bison, and a range of other mammals being preyed upon by humans.

The large mammals so depicted, and whose butchered bones are found within the caves, would have moved together in herds across an open tundra landscape. They would also have been present in smaller groups and as individuals in the birch and pine zones, but, moving towards the thickest broadleaf woodland, the density of large mammals would have fallen off. So an obvious place for the contemporary humans is within the predator level of the open tundra ecological pyramid, and we would then envisage those human populations moving back and forward with this vegetation zone. Indeed, we can follow the tundra belt today, and find humans who are still stalking reindeer in modern Lapland.

The story is not as simple as that. If it were, there would be no humans left in the densely wooded island that Britain had become by the sixth millennium BC. It would instead have been left to the birds, rodents and

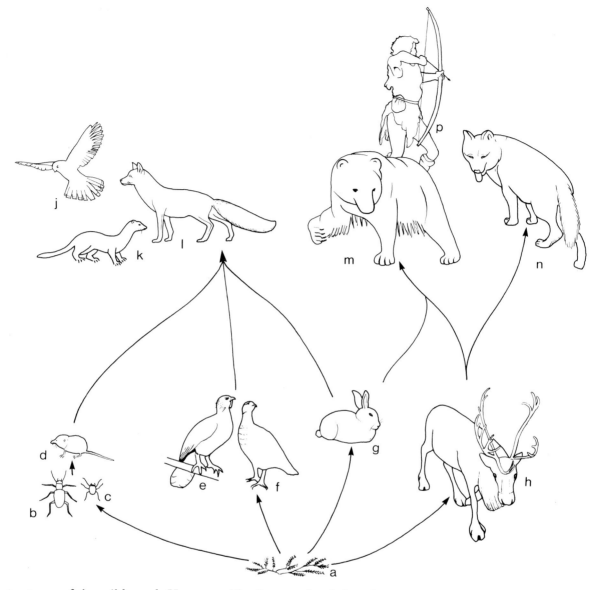

creatures of the wildwood. However, like foxes and red deer, humans are versatile animals. By modifying their eating habits they can switch from one ecological pyramid to another. There is ample archaeological evidence that humans stayed in this country as the zone of open, cold climate vegetation retreated up mountains and to the north.

In staying put, they tipped various of the delicate balances we have been exploring in this chapter, with a dramatic and lasting effect on the landscape. To see how these balances were tipped we must focus on particular human communities that lived in and around the wildwood, and the evidence they left behind.

Figure 9 A food chain on an early Flandrian heath:
a) crowberry heath;
b, c) various invertebrates;
d) pigmy shrew; e) capercailzie;
f) red grouse; g) mountain hare; h) reindeer; j) birds of prey; k) stoat; l) fox;
m) bear; n) wolf; p) human.

3

Breaking ground and tipping the balance

In the last chapter, the European environment of the Quaternary Epoch was portrayed as a dynamic and delicately balanced system, in which all species move towards an equilibrium state with each other, and with their environment. Within this system, changes in any one factor can have a knock-on effect throughout the system. So, for example, each slight increase in temperature after the last glaciation has forced whole communities of plants and animals, linked together within an intricate food web, to more northerly latitudes, and to higher altitudes. In the course of these movements, some species became stranded on islands and up high mountains, sometimes severely reducing their chances of survival.

Even before the glacier's final retreat, such forces had removed the bison, woolly rhino, cave bear, cave lion, hyena and giant deer from the English land surface. Less vulnerable animals such as the reindeer successfully moved with the tundra belt northwards to Lapland, no doubt followed by the humans that preyed upon them.

With these forces in operation, and with all the plants and animals in the tundra ecological pyramid moving northward, we would not have been surprised were England to have lost its human population as the dense broadleaved wildwood established itself. Yet the converse of this has happened. The human population has remained and become firmly established, and England has in the process lost its wildwood.

Somewhere along the line, the delicate ecological balance seems to have been tipped. At some stage the natural progression through the various stages of woodland has taken a new course. It is to this change of course that we shall now turn.

HUNTER-GATHERERS IN NORTH YORKSHIRE

We must start by focusing in more closely on those humans that, rather than follow the tundra herds northwards, remained to eke out a living within the birch woodland that was engulfing the land. An area well suited to examining the human populations that inhabited the encroaching birchwoods of the ninth and eighth millennia BC is the Vale of Pickering in Yorkshire.

Today this vale is an area of agricultural land. Looking southwards from the heart of the vale, the brow of the Yorkshire Wolds rises steeply

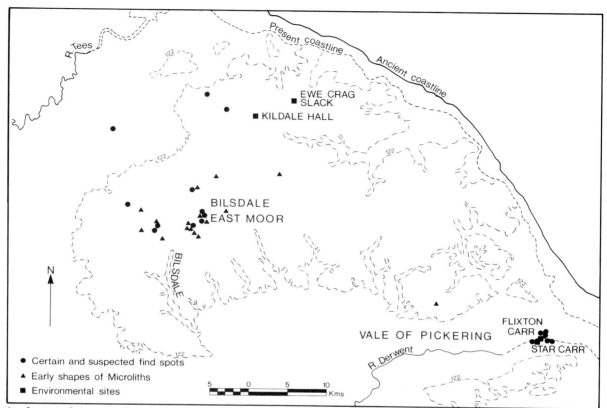

Figure 10 The Vale of Pickering and the North Yorkshire Moors, showing sites mentioned in the text together with findspots of early post-glacial artefacts (after R. Jacobi and R. Jones).

in front of us. Looking northwards the foothills of the North York Moors rise up above the string of villages situated along their base. To the east a low ridge of hills extends towards the coast. The hills around us are clothed with a patchwork of cereals, pasture and conifer plantations, and the vale itself is fully cultivated. Beneath our feet and all along the dykes that dissect the vale, we see the jet black peat that has preserved evidence of the Vale of Pickering in a much earlier epoch.

One of the things we can learn by examining the peats and lake muds below us is that when the hillslopes around were being engulfed by the early post-glacial birchwood, the Vale of Pickering was a lake.

The view from the centre of this early post-glacial lake would have been quite different from today's view. Instead of today's agricultural landscape, the slopes would have been thick with a delicate green birch canopy, the blanket of trees merging into the lake's dense, reedy margin. Up beyond the northern horizon, the birch woodland would have fragmented into ever diminishing clumps, as we moved towards the distant snow-capped moor.

In the summer months we might find small bands of humans lighting their campfires along the fragmented upper margin of the birchwood. Under the cover of their temporary hide shelters, hunting arrows would be manufactured from slender wooden shafts tipped with freshly chipped flint flakes. As they worked away on their flint cores and fed on fresh venison, steak and bone marrow, they would discuss their strategy for the next day's hunt. In contrast to their ancestors of the open tundra, who depended on a knowledge of the large migrating herds, these humans had to anticipate the movements of the smaller groups of wild cattle, deer and elk scattered through the woodland stretching out below them. It would not be easy to seek out and kill these animals, and they would not be able to do it with bows and arrows alone.

One of their major handicaps was their heavy dependence on eyesight, the keenest human sense, and one which, while well adapted to the open tundra, is of limited use in dense woodland. What is needed here is a good sense of smell. At some stage, humans had gone into a kind of partnership with another major predator which did have a keen sense of smell – the wolf, or, in its domesticated form, the dog – and a small group of dogs would be with them at the campsite. They would be taken on the hunt and used to track the prey, in order that their human companions knew where to let loose with bows and arrows.

Alongside this partnership, another advantage humans had in woodland hunting was their ability to start fires. The smoke from a good burn towards the treeline would flush the prey out into open areas, where they were ready targets for an adept archer. Once wounded and sufficiently incapacitated to be caught by the relatively slow-moving humans, the prey could be killed with a spear plunged deep into its lungs.

The largest deer in the wildwood may have weighed in excess of 200kg (440lb), and the wild cattle would have been several times larger again. These animals would need to be chopped up into manageable pieces before being taken from the kill-site within the woodland or clearing to a distant base-camp. The animal would therefore be skinned with a razor-sharp flint blade, and the limb joints pummelled with a flint chopper to detach them from the body. In this way small bands of humans dispersed within the woodland, especially along its borders, could gather stocks of meat-bearing limbs and jawbones, hides and antlers to take back to base-camp.

To reach their destination, the dogs and humans laden with prey would in some cases have to trek for several days down the North Yorkshire dales through unaccommodating woodland. At certain times of year they would assemble far below the treeline along the margins of the Pickering lake. Here trees would be felled to form working platforms on which the gathered skins could be treated, the meat smoked and dried, and the antlers fashioned into tips for harpoons and spears for the following season's hunting.

This picture can be reconstructed entirely from what survives in the archaeological record. It is still possible to find and excavate the scorched surfaces on which the campfires along the treeline were lit, and recover the adjacent scatters of flint flakes that arrow manufacture had generated. Two such sites have been excavated up on Bilsdale East Moor to the north of the lake. We can follow one of the routes they would have taken to reach the lakeside camps, only today we can do it in the comfort of a car along the B1257!

The lake muds in the vale itself preserve the pollen from which the birchwood may be reconstructed, and in places the pollen grains are accompanied by large numbers of minute fragments of charcoal, the kind that makes up smoke dust from a forest fire. A flush of such charcoal has been recorded at the birchwood level of the peats at Flixton, just south of Scarborough.

Close to Flixton lies the best known archaeological site in the Vale, Star Carr. Here, the lake muds and peats have preserved a birch platform littered with the debris of skin preparation and antler-working, together with a range of meat bones, dominated by the limb and jaw bones that were brought preferentially back to the camp. Some of the bones are heavily fractured, as a result of breakage to release marrow and bone grease. In among these bones was a fragment of the skull of one of the domestic dogs used in the hunt.

These sites provide us with a valuable picture of hunting activities in the early post-glacial birchwood. They indicate how the use of dogs, fire, and hunting and trapping equipment might have compensated for the human's lack of agility and poor sense of smell, features that, without compensation, would have excluded human predators from a woodland ecosystem.

Evidence from these sites points to yet another way in which these human groups adapted to the woodland environment. We can see from the animal bones they discarded that, while their tundra-dwelling ancestors tended to concentrate their efforts on particular species of large mammal, the occupants of Star Carr had had to move to a more diverse diet. In addition to elk, red deer, roe deer and wild cattle, the list includes marten, hedgehog, hare, badger, fox, beaver, and such birds as grebe, crane, stork, merganser, diver and pintail. It would seem that these humans were coming to terms with the smaller, more dispersed groups of prey within a wildwood, by catching and eating a much wider range of animals.

It is rather difficult to say whether the same thing was true for plant foods; few plants leave anything as clear cut as a chopped or chewed bone in the archaeological record. We can recover pollen and seeds from the waterlogged deposits around the lake margin, and from these can speculate that the hunters of wild cattle and deer were also gathering for food the inner bark of pine, the tubers of water-lily, the fruits and nuts of hawthorn, crowberry and hazel, and the sugary sap of birch and reed. They may also have been gathering wild honey from the surrounding woods.

In this way the North Yorkshire sites provide us with evidence of the way in which humans were able to adapt to the encroaching birchwood and move into a different ecological pyramid, by adopting new methods of food procurement, and by forming new relationships with other species within that pyramid. However, these same adaptations that allowed humans to remain within the encroaching woodland ecosystem would eventually lead to the delicate ecological balance of those woodland ecosystems being irrevocably tipped. In order to see how, we

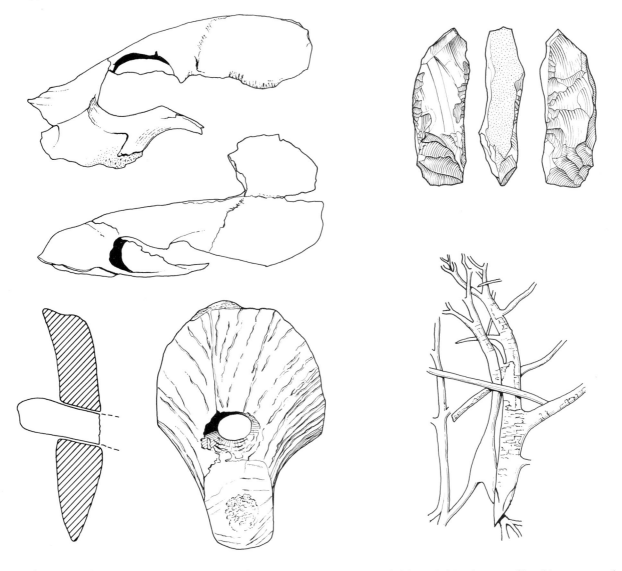

Figure 11 Possible human intervention in the ecosystem; evidence from Star Carr. *Above left*: fragmentary skull of a domesticated dog; *below left*: hafted antler 'mattock-head', used perhaps for digging; *above right*: flint implement, possibly for chopping wood; *below right*: hewn birch trunk laying among felled branches on the site.

must take the various human activities within the woodland in turn, and consider what impact they might have. We start with the most obvious impact, the felling of trees.

Felling and digging

The flint and bone debris at Star Carr overlay a platform of felled birch. Among this wood was a birch trunk over 8m (26ft) in length, its base hewn into a pencil-like stump. Such timbers provide dramatic evidence of the ability of the site's occupants to fell quite large trees with the aid of a small stone axe, examples of which are found on contemporary sites throughout the country. We can imagine tree-felling in this way having an impact on the immediate environment, by creating local clearances, but the long-term ecological influence of felling is easily over-emphasised.

As it is a living, dynamic entity, woodland cannot be dismantled like a piece of scaffolding, and the removal of trunks need have little structural influence in the long term. The characteristic trees of the English wildwood either grow back quickly from stumps, or reseed themselves with ease. Many of the small woodlands of today's landscape have been felled or 'coppiced' a hundred times or more over the centuries. It is only when their roots are grubbed out that they cease to regenerate.

There is some evidence that the occupants of Star Carr were rooting around in the soils near the site. The excavations produced a number of implements fashioned from antler bases, which were worked into a pointed tip and hafted. It seems reasonable to describe them as mattocks or hoes, but whether they were involved in the grubbing out of roots is an open question. The New Zealand Maoris used hoes, not only to dig up wild roots and rhizomes, but also to encourage the growth of bracken, whose rhizomes they ate. It may be that something similar took place around Star Carr. In any case, the presence of plants of disturbed ground, such as docks, fathen, chickweed and stinging nettles, on the site does suggest that soils were being disturbed for some purpose. What can be said is that, like the felling of trees with stone axes, the grubbing out of roots with antler hoes would have been a fairly slow process.

So the ability to chop down large trees may be more significant in terms of using timber than creating open spaces. There are other ways in which a small amount of human effort can have a much larger impact on the environment, such as the use of fire.

Burning

There is no underwood saving in swamps and low grounds that are wet . . . for it being in the custom of the Indians to burne the wood in November, when the grasse is withered, and the leaves dryed, it consumes all the underwood and rubbish which otherwise would overgrow the country, making it unpassable, and spoil their much affected hunting; so that by this means in those places where the Indians inhabit there is scarce a brush or bramble, or any combersome underwood to be seene in the more champion ground.

Those lines, written of Massachusetts Bay by a seventeenth-century explorer give us some idea of the degree to which hunter-gatherers can influence a temperate woodland ecosystem by the use of fire. In fact a number of sixteenth- and seventeenth-century explorers of the New World attest to the extent of burning, and the subsequent opening up of the vegetation.

The impact of burning lies, of course, in the ease with which it can spread. Fire can certainly open up far larger areas than the act of felling alone, but the long-term effect may not be dissimilar. In the same way that a felled woodland will soon revert to its normal form, so will a freshly burnt woodland revert through a series of stages to its original state.

In the spring following the fire, a rich cover of green herbage will take hold, attracting grazing animals to collect on the open ground. The degree to which this browse can be increased in this way has been measured after forest fires in the woodlands of North America. The sheer weight of edible browse in a particular patch of ground can increase by a factor of up to ten in the first two years following a burn. This in turn may lead to a doubling, or even trebling, of the numbers of deer gathering to graze on that patch. It was for this effect on the grazing animals as much as to improve visibility and drive out game that the Amerindian hunters made extensive use of fire. The same was no doubt true of the woodland hunters of early post-glacial England.

These first few seasons after the fire would be favourable ones in terms of hunting, but the process of ecological succession would not freeze at that point. In periods when the grazing pressure was relaxed, thorny shrubs and brambles would grab the chance to establish themselves and develop into a thick undergrowth. Their thorns would protect the young regrowth of hazel from subsequent grazing, and these would develop into sizeable trees. This stage would favour gathering rather than hunting, and provide the human population with hazelnuts and berries of bramble, haw and sloe. A few years later the larger trees would begin to shade out this prolific undergrowth, and the woodland would return to its earlier state.

This would be the end of the story, were it not for the fact that the extensive impact of fire can be so easily repeated. An area that is reburnt every few years may fail ever to complete its normal succession. It may instead get suspended in an intermediate state.

The pollen record for the English wildwood provides a great deal of evidence that such an intermediate state was commonplace. The evidence for this is the frequently erratic behaviour in the curve for hazel pollen, which will often rise to sharp peaks. Such rises are found directly above both the Star Carr birchwood platform, and the Flixton Carr charcoal layer. The hazel peaks at these and many other sites suggest a patchwork of regenerating clearances, many at the stage of a shrubby hazel thicket. Indeed the hunter-gatherers who set the woodland ablaze may have been rewarded more by protein in the form of hazelnuts than by protein on the hoof.

With the practice of repeated burning we can begin to see a sustained and tangible influence on the resilient wildwood. But even this practice, however dramatic its immediate impact, only modified rather than removed the wildwood. The processes that had this effect were more subtle, and involved the removal, not of massive trunks, but of tender young shoots.

Grazing

A tree growing in the wild has a natural lifespan. As it reaches a certain size and a certain age, the foliage will be hard-pushed to catch enough of the sun's energy to maintain its massive bulk. The branches will die back in turn and the trunk hollow out, and eventually the tree will succumb to competition, or simply die of old age. So the survival of every species, however massive in its mature form, is dependent on the renewed growth of young green seedlings or suckers, which in turn are extremely vulnerable to grazing.

In a stable woodland ecosystem, the numbers of grazing animals tend to level out below densities that would lead to the destruction of their woodland food-source. The young shoots do manage to re-establish, and the small clearing created by a dying tree does eventually regenerate to closed woodland, and the grazers do disperse to seek out further clearings.

The woodland ecosystem may in this way remain stable, but it is at a very vulnerable point. If the grazing intensity is for any reason increased beyond that equilibrium level, then the pressure on the new generation of seedlings or suckers may be more than the ecosystem can bear. A further crucial point about grazing is that while felling, uprooting or burning may occur as isolated events, grazing animals don't stop eating; grazing is a continuous, relentless, ecological force. While the felling of trees is the most obvious agent of deforestation, and burning the most dramatic, the sustained nibbling of young shoots is undoubtedly the most powerful. Just as overgrazing today has the power to extend the boundaries of today's deserts, so did it have the power to open areas of prehistoric woodland.

To see how stable grazing can turn to overgrazing, we must put together all the factors outlined above. If we assume that human hunters were aware that their prey would tend to gather in natural woodland clearings, and that similar clearings could be created by the use of fire, then it seems likely that they would encourage and create such clearings. It could further be suggested that, when the clearing became too overgrown with thorny shrubs, the humans might burn it back in order that the visits by grazing animals would not cease, and the clearing be maintained. If this were the case, the abundance of browse that sprung in a young clearance would gradually decline in the artificially sustained clearance, and a natural response might be to 'enrich' the clearing with browse imported from the adjacent, thick woodland.

At this point, the speculation can be linked with archaeological evidence. The study of pollen from early sites associated with human activity at Oakhanger in Hampshire, and Winfrith Heath in Dorset, has revealed quantities of ivy pollen that are remarkably high, and far higher than could be explained in terms of its natural agencies alone. The simplest explanation of these high pollen counts is that these hunter-gatherers were gathering leaf-laden ivy branches in some quantity, presumably for animal browse.

In a sense, adding browse to a sustained clearing is no different from charging an animal trap with bait – a practice which may well have considerable antiquity. Its significance here is that it involves an interference with the food chain, that is the very workings of the ecological pyramid, and it is such interference that is likely to have the most significant effect on the ecosystem.

Stable and unstable ecosystems

In many cases, the activities outlined above would simply have prolonged the process of vegetation succession. The sustained clearing would eventually return to a fully wooded condition, if after a longer duration. In some cases a more permanent change would occur, for example where exposure had some effect on the underlying soils.

There are a number of instances where the presence of post-glacial hunter-gatherers is associated with soil erosion. One such example is the site of Flixton on the Vale of Pickering. Here, alongside the pollen grains of hazel and specks of charcoal that have already been discussed, the peat sediments contained a lens of sand that had washed in from the adjacent slopes. The association of these three pieces of evidence, and the knowledge that hunter-gatherers were active throughout this area, lead us to ask whether this erosion was caused by the maintenance of woodland clearings and the related lack of consolidation by tree roots.

A similar example is provided by a hunter-gatherer site on a sandy knoll at Shippea Hill in Cambridgeshire. The knoll lies adjacent to a deep accumulation of peat, and this peat contains evidence, both of the chipped flint artefacts disgarded by the occupants of the knoll, and of the eroded sand that accompanied those artefacts. In addition, the pollen collected from the peat above and below this sandy lens displays a very marked pattern.

Below the sandy lens, the pollen is dominated by pine and hazel. Above the lens, the pollen assemblage is quite different, and alder and lime are the dominant trees. As we have seen, there is nothing unusual about a shift from pine/hazel to broadleaf woodland; it is part of the normal process of post-glacial succession.

What is interesting is the clear coincidence of the vegetation change with the period of human disturbance. It is as if, in an ecosystem becoming susceptible to change, the added stress of human interference hurried that change along. Such an idea finds support in numerous other instances where evidence for the activity of hunter-gatherers lies precisely at a point of change in an environmental sequence. The sites around the Vale of Pickering, for example, lie broadly at the point of transition between birch woodland and pine/hazel woodland.

Such an instability of ecosystems at a point of transition would apply, not only through time, but also through space. It will be remembered that some of the North Yorkshire sites discussed above were located at the treeline, the highest altitude that can support a woodland, and that much hunting activity would have been focused on this treeline. At this transitional point between woodland and open ground, the effect of sustaining clearances would have been gradually to break up the marginal woodland and depress the treeline downslope.

The effect of a mosaic of sustained clearances within the post-glacial wildwood would thus be different in different places. In the most resilient wildwood, their effect would be limited to the delay of normal succession, and an encouragement of species that thrive in the intermediate stages of succession. In zones of transition, either in space or in time, and over soils vulnerable to modification and erosion, these sustained clearances may well have tipped the ecosystem across that transition, in some cases removing the woodland cover on a fairly permanent basis.

Humans and other species: changing relationships

Returning to the open glade to which branches of ivy were brought, this addition of leafy fodder to the natural browse signals a change, not just in the direction of ecological succession, but also in the relationship between predator and prey. Many hunter-gatherers in the past would have concerned themselves only with the gathered plants and slain animals. For them the art of survival lay in the ability to locate resources and in the skill of the hunt. The gathering of fodder for animals is something quite different; it reflects an involvement in animals as a resource while those animals are still alive.

This critical shift in attitude towards the species on which humans were dependent lies behind one of the most fundamental influences they have had on the ecosystem. By concerning themselves with how those plants and animals lived, as well as how they died, humans have influenced the health, behaviour and even the genetic makeup of several such species. To see how this could happen, we can follow the example of the dogs that hunted with those early humans in North Yorkshire.

From wolves to dogs

It seems likely that the bond between dogs and humans is far older than the dog skull found at Star Carr. The human hunters of the open tundra would have repeatedly come into close contact with wolves. They would have seen them as they lay in waiting to ambush herds of migrating reindeer. The humans would wait at mountain passes and at fording points along rivers to catch the herd by surprise. The wolves would follow the herd from behind, picking off the slower runners. After the frenzy of slaughter, the two predators would meet again as the wolves lingered around the human campsites to pick off discarded scraps from the kill. As the two species have home ranges of a similar size, it would often be the same groups of humans and wolves that came into contact.

We can speculate that the relationship between the two predators became one of cooperation rather than competition. Such cooperation between species is by no means unheard of. Indeed wolves may be seen today in some parts of the Arctic region behaving 'cooperatively' with ravens. The ravens' facility of aerial surveillance leads the wolves to a herd of reindeer, and as the wolves move in for the kill, the ravens hover in waiting to demolish the scraps of carcass left by the pack.

In the case of wolves and humans, we can imagine that the two species gradually developed a 'social' bond, such as they still share throughout the world. Where that bond entailed breeding of the animals 'in captivity', we might assume pronounced changes to their genetic makeup; selection pressures in captivity could be quite different from such pressures in the wild. Wolves with large teeth and snout would gradually become domestic dogs, with smaller teeth and snout, such as was found on the skull specimen from Star Carr.

As traditional hunting patterns continued, this bond may have remained purely social in nature, as is still the case between aborigines and dingoes in Australia. However, as the encroachment of woodland transformed the post-glacial land surface, so, as we have seen, did this bond confer a considerable ecological advantage.

As has already been mentioned, cooperation between species is not uncommon. The biologist's term is 'symbiosis', which means 'living together', and it is a term that may be applied to a whole range of partnerships, from humans and dogs, wolves and ravens, ants and aphids, to the fungus and microscopic plant that go together to form a lichen. From a purely human standpoint, this kind of bond with another species is often described as taming, or domestication, that is bringing species within the domestic sphere. Such a process of domestication has transformed our relationship with the environment, as we have progressively tamed a greater number of species within it.

To appreciate the full impact of domestication on the English landscape, we must shift our attention from the small bands of dogs and humans feeding along a chilly woodland edge in north-west Europe, to a contemporary group of humans that were feeding along another woodland edge in much warmer climes.

HUMAN ECOSYSTEMS OF THE NEAR EAST

We have seen how the North Yorkshire hunters occupied a landscape which was progressively becoming engulfed in woodland. We could follow that story right across Europe, and see northern England at the north-western extreme of a massive spread of woodland punctuated only by water and high mountains. Moving eastwards from the Hungarian Plain, where seasonal extremes of temperature and aridity curbed the succession to full woodland, we would begin to see the eastern margin of this enormous spread break up into open areas.

In the Near East itself, these open areas coalesced into vast expanses, dominated by herbs and small plants that could complete their growth within a single season. When the season was warm and moist summers these areas of steppe vegetation would form a lush green carpet peppered with colourful annuals. A few months later, when the moisture had gone and the temperature was moving between extremes, the steppe would be transformed into an array of brittle, brown and amber stems, all life and energy expended into hardened, dry seed heads.

At around the time that dogs and humans were skirting the boundary between woodland and heath in North Yorkshire, the Near Eastern boundary between woodland and steppe was also a focus of human activity. Some of the potential resources were the same here as in Yorkshire; wild pigs and wild cattle occurred right across Europe and the Near East. There would also be differences; our woods contained hazelnuts and brambles, in the woods of the Near East we might have found pistachios and almonds. The open areas beyond the woodland edge would also be rich sources of food. Those dry seeds of the steppe could be pounded and cracked, then moistened and cooked. They are the ancestors of our modern wheat and barley.

Up above the 'fields' of wild cereals the hunters would seek out two slender mountain creatures, distinguished by their elegant, curved horns. These animals, the mouflon and the bezoar, are the ancestors of our modern sheep and goats.

These ecosystems were rich in potential human food. The yield of wild grass seeds from them was quite comparable with the yields of some of the wheat-fields of much later epochs. Not only could these grass seeds be gathered with ease, they could also be moved around and stored with ease. The mouflons and bezoars lent themselves not only to being hunted, but also to being maintained in captivity. We can see that this was happening at an early stage by the presence of bones from very young animals in early settlements, something that would only be seen if the animals were being born within those settlements.

Because of the control the humans could exercise over their resources, they could be moved around. A band of humans could migrate with its animals and stock of seeds for replanting, just as their northern contemporaries could migrate together with their dogs. The difference between the two was that, while one group had brought a companion and co-predator into the domestic sphere, the other group had succeeded in domesticating a substantial part of its food chain. That portable food chain is what we now describe as agriculture.

THE SPREAD OF AGRICULTURE ACROSS EUROPE

By around 7000 BC, this portable food chain is in evidence in various parts of southern Europe, particularly in the Balkan Peninsular. We can detect its presence by looking at charred seeds and animal bones. During the sixth millennium BC, these remains also begin to appear in settlements further to the north and west. We can follow this spread along Europe's valleys and plains, where the new plants and animals would have been reared in clearings within an unfamiliar woodland. These pioneering farmers were not just spreading their crops and animals; they were also inadvertently spreading other components of the steppe ecosystem. The seeds of such plants as black bindweed, tare and corn cockle travelled from the Near East as seed impurities to join a growing list of agricultural weeds.

The spread of this portable food chain was slow. Not until at least 2000 years after its first appearance in Europe was it to progress beyond the valleys and plains of temperate Europe, finally to reach England's shores.

Agriculture within the English landscape

The first hint of agriculture within England's landscape comes in the first half of the fifth millennium BC, with the appearance of a trace of cereal pollen at one or two sites. Their appearance is not accompanied by any other marked change in the pollen record; it seems that their initial addition to a woodland ecosystem that had been battered about by millennia of felling, burning and grazing was relatively inconspicuous. Each temporarily open plot planted with cereals would soon revert to woodland on abandonment. The sheep and goats would join the other feeders along the woodland edge.

Yet the previous millennia in Europe had shown how agricultural communities tended slowly but steadily to expand and spread. With grazing populations being maintained by their human protectors rather than by their own food source, and an artificial vegetation being maintained within woodland clearings, it was only a question of time before the wildwood had difficulty in fully bouncing back to its former self. Around half a millennium after the first appearance of cereals in England, we can detect in pollen sequences woodland openings that last centuries rather than years, in some cases remaining open permanently.

It was at this time that the combined pressures on the wildwood claimed a major victim; native elms were never again to regain their wildwood status, and this episode is marked on pollen diagrams as the Elm Decline mentioned in the first chapter.

After several millennia of clearing trees and breaking ground, the balance had finally been tipped, and the wildwood was subsequently to share England's land surface with vast stretches of agricultural landscape. We can now move on to examine the form those new agricultural landscapes took.

4

A landscape of ancestors

In the centuries that followed the Elm Decline, the plants and animals that had been brought across Europe from the Near East were to transform the landscape. Where once ageing trees crowded around England's riverbanks, wheat and barley now grew. The woodland edge, which had retreated from the rivers' margins, was grazed not just by deer, but by goats too, and cattle and pigs had also been brought into the domestic sphere.

Along the open ground that lined the river courses we would have seen a patchwork of cultivated plots, rough pasture, spreads of bracken and reverting scrub. Sheep would be grazing, and nearby we might see the overgrown turf being torn up by a wooden 'rip-ard' fashioned from a single oak tree and drawn by two domestic cattle, much smaller animals than their wild counterparts in the nearby wood. In the wake of the ard, other members of the farming family would be hammering at the broken clods with hoes of wood or antler, to prepare a tilth for next year's cereals. Once this work was done, they could return to the preparation of the massive earthen monument they were building in honour of the community's dead.

Most components of this scene would soon go the way of all organic materials and leave no trace to posterity, but the earthen monument would remain; such 'barrows' form a conspicuous part of our modern landscape. Beneath this barrow a slab of ground would be also be preserved, a fragmentary snapshot of an ancient landscape long since disappeared.

It might be that the barrow was erected over a disused cereal plot, and the snapshot might preserve the criss-cross scratches of the rip-ard in the subsoil. Some of the plants and small animals that flourished in and around the plot may have left pollen and skeletal fragments to be sealed beneath the monument.

Once the human population had embarked on this practice of erecting large durable monuments in the landscape, a development that took place at around the time of the Elm Decline, they inadvertently left us with a supplementary source of information about early landscapes. For preceding periods, our environmental picture is based predominantly on the general pollen rain arriving in lake sediments and peat bogs. Thereafter, the newly established activity of monument building enriches that picture by providing countless snapshots in the form of

Figure 12 Map of locations
cited in Chapter 4.

buried land surfaces. In this chapter we examine the early agricultural landscapes that can be inferred from them. First we must consider what survives in a soil that has been buried for thousands of years.

BURIED LAND SURFACES

The closer to the surface a buried object is, the more vulnerable it is to processes of weathering and decay. While conditions such as moisture and temperature are relatively stable deep down, the upper layers of the soil experience cycles of wetting and drying, and of freezing and thawing, which place physical stress on any contained object. While the deeper layers are penetrated only by burrowing animals and the more penetrating roots, the upper layers of soil teem with life, and biological breakdown is accordingly fast.

So in building a monument of earth or stone, and thereby burying a land surface, anything on that buried surface is immediately removed from the most vulnerable zone of the soil. According to how deeply the surface is buried, the things so preserved can range from the foundations of a building to the biological contents of the soil itself. The turf within the massive mound of Silbury Hill in Wiltshire was sufficiently well buried to preserve even the delicate summer wings of a flying ant.

To see the kind of information that can be gleaned from buried land surfaces in more detail, we can move to a much slighter monument, a little over 1 km ($\frac{5}{8}$ mile) to the north-west of Silbury Hill, lying on South Street on the outskirts of the village of Avebury.

The South Street Long Barrow

This earthen monument would have once stood proud above the ground surface, like the prominent West Kennet Long Barrow that lies 2 km ($1\frac{1}{4}$ miles) to the south-east of the site. Centuries of agriculture have honed it down to a far less conspicuous feature, but one which nevertheless seals a very informative land surface.

Immediately below the chalk rubble and turf of the mound, excavation revealed a grey loamy layer which was an ancient soil, buried when the mound was built over 5000 years ago. Here and there, scatters of oak charcoal bear witness to fires lit immediately before the mound was erected. Below this surface, the top few centimetres of soil were free of stones and the larger chalk fragments. Such stone-free layers are known as 'worm-sorted' layers: they result from fine sediments passing through worms' guts and accumulating at the surface. Such worm-sorted layers will only survive in the absence of cultivation, and they consequently provide an indication of uncultivated ground.

Below this worm-sorted layer were two concentrations of chipped flint, debris from earlier episodes of tool manufacture. These in turn overlay a band of soil that was fully mixed, in the manner of a cultivated soil. Scored into the chalky subsoil below was the direct imprint of cultivation. The criss-cross pattern of shallow grooves at a spacing of about 30cm (12in) is what we would expect to result from the kind of rip-ard mentioned at the beginning of this chapter.

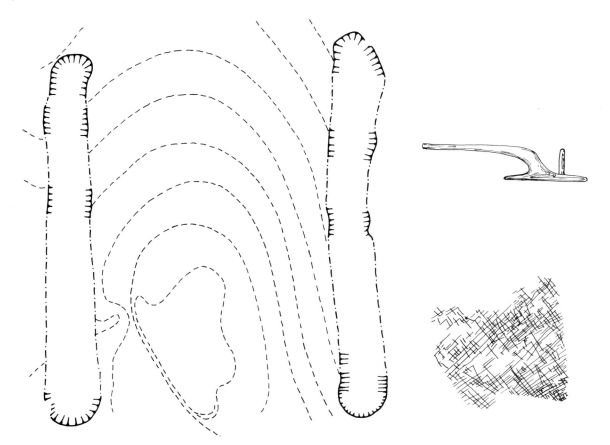

Figure 13 The South Street Long Barrow. *Left*: schematic plan of barrow; *below right*: cultivation marks beneath barrow (both adapted from P. Ashbee *et al.* 1979 *PPS* 45); *above right*: a crook ard.

The ard is a cultivation tool which is still in use in many parts of the world. It simply tears through the turf, rather than turning it over in the manner of our modern ploughs. Because it only tears the turf, ard-cultivated fields are typically tilled in two directions, generating the criss-cross pattern visible under the South Street Long Barrow. After breaking up an overgrown plot with a heavy rip-ard, a lighter ard would have been used for year to year cultivation, reaching less deeply and leaving no marks on the subsoil.

Below the cultivation marks under the barrow are the hollows left by tree roots long since decayed, and the swirling patterns left by the thermal distortion of the chalk bedrock caused by the low temperatures of the last glaciation.

This sequence of contrasting stages of land use shows how much can be gleaned from buried land surfaces. We can infer from the simple observations outlined above that after the last glaciation the site of South Street developed a tree cover, which was subsequently replaced by cultivated land. After cultivation ceased there were a few instances of flint tool production, a phase without cultivation, leading to the development of a worm-sorted layer, and the burning of a few fires prior to the erection of a long barrow.

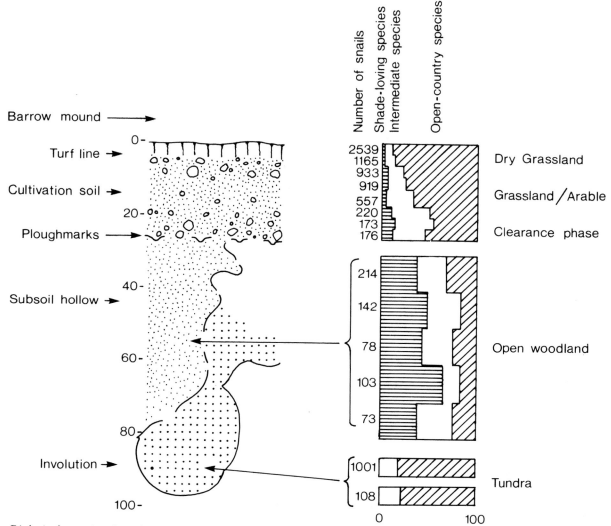

Barrow mound ⟶

Turf line →

Cultivation soil →

Ploughmarks ⟶

Subsoil hollow →

Involution →

Number of snails
Shade-loving species
Intermediate species
Open-country species

2539
1165
933
919
557
220
173
176

Dry Grassland

Grassland/Arable

Clearance phase

214
142
78
103
73

Open woodland

1001
108

Tundra

Figure 14 Schematic section through South Street Long Barrow (after J. G. Evans)

Biological remains from buried soils

Pollen is not particularly well preserved in the dry alkaline soil beneath the South Street Long Barrow, and what does survive will have been mixed up by the earthworms that we can see in certain periods thrived in that soil. Even so, Geoffrey Dimbleby has managed to make some sense of the pollen from the soil buried beneath this and a number of other prehistoric mounds in the vicinity. He has shown that, although the land beneath these mounds was open and in some cases cultivated, the wildwood was never far away; over a third of the pollen grains from South Street were from trees rather than herbs. He also found bracken spores in large quantities, giving a tentative impression of the appearance of land recently released from cultivation.

Because this buried soil is dry and alkaline, it lends itself to the study of another biological component – snail shells. As we saw in Chapter 1 in the account of the nearby site of Fyfield Down, an analysis of these shells can help us to detect the transition from woodland to open land on soils over the chalk. John Evans' work on this material also allows us to distinguish between the different phases of open land at South Street. In the well-mixed soil above the cultivation marks, a common species is *Pupilla muscorum*, which is characteristic of unstable, partly vegetated surfaces, such as we would expect in a cultivated field. This species is far less common in the worm-sorted layer above, which, instead, is richer in species characteristic of short grassland.

The slab of land buried beneath the South Street Long Barrow provides a detailed, but very localised, picture of the early agricultural landscape. We can, for example, detect the traces of a cultivated plot, the snails that could withstand the annual churning of the ard, the woodland that the plot replaced, and the bracken that invaded once cultivation had ceased. Yet we cannot say how representative that small area of land surface is of the broader landscape of which it was once part.

What we can do is complement the data with evidence from other monuments that lie within a short distance. In the case of the South Street Long Barrow, several such monuments may be found within a few kilometres.

Sites in the vicinity of South Street

Beneath the Beckhampton Long Barrow, no more than 3km (1¾ miles) to the south-west, the sequence following woodland clearance is quite different. The nature of the soil, and its contained pollen and snails, go together to indicate that, although cultivation took place nearby, the pre-barrow soil was for several centuries an area of open, uncultivated grassland.

Buried soil studies have also been conducted at the West Kennet Long Barrow and on a series of earthworks on the nearby Windmill Hill. Taken together, the snapshots provided by the soils buried beneath each of these broadly contemporary monuments can be pieced together to form the picture of the patchwork landscape with which this chapter began.

The nearby sites have more to offer than buried soils alone. Meat bones have been found in large quantities during excavation, piled up in the ditches of the Windmill Hill enclosure, together with the charred seeds of the occasional cereal that fell into the fire. Other grains that fell onto the potter's working surface have left casts that are both durable and recognisable in the cooking pots that lie broken in deposits of this age. From these we can discern the crops that were planted in those early riverside plots, and the animals that grazed in the rough pasture and along the woodland edge.

Seeds and bones of the farming food chain

Although the range of domestic animals kept – cattle, pigs, sheep, and goats – was similar to that of today, early farm animals would have been different in stature and appearance. Most were smaller than their modern counterparts, and sheep and pigs had different coats and were of different shapes.

The closest parallel to a prehistoric sheep is the Soay sheep, named after the St Kilda island on which over the last two millennia it has escaped breed 'improvement'. We can see these slender, agile sheep at the Cotswold Wildlife Park, and at the reconstructed prehistoric farm at Butser Hill, near Petersfield. Their coats are of various shades of beige and brown, and their wool is moulted, and therefore plucked rather than shorn.

The snub-nosed, pink-skinned pigs of today would not have been seen in prehistory, or even in the Middle Ages. Medieval illustrations sometimes depict the bristly coat, long snout, and longer legs of earlier pigs. Indeed, they would have been closer to their wild boar ancestors, both in appearance, and in the much less intensive way in which they were managed in early farming communities.

The main crops were wheat and barley, though these too were of different types to today's crops. Our modern 'bread wheats' were occasionally grown, but other species were generally favoured that were hardier in the face of attack by fungi and birds, and of competition with weeds. Foremost among these was 'emmer wheat', a species that today is confined to some of the remotest parts, such as the Ethiopian Highlands and the Turkish-Russian border.

We can see emmer wheat growing nearer to home, where it has been replanted at the Butser Hill Ancient Farm. With its smooth, shining husks and long awns, it is rather more elegant than modern wheat. It also has a higher protein content and is held to produce a superior flour. In fact, it is not entirely clear why we stopped growing such an appealing crop! Its popularity certainly lasted for several thousand years, and only declined during the first millennium BC, when agricultural methods were changing on many fronts.

Some of the plots contained yet another species of wheat, even further removed from our modern forms. The diminutive heads of 'einkorn wheat' are little different in size from many wild grasses. Indeed, this plant is very close genetically to the wild wheats of the Near Eastern steppe that generated our broad array of domesticated forms; it would take an expert eye to tell them apart.

As well as wheats there would be barleys; not the slender two-row barleys so well suited to the requirements of modern brewing, but the fatter six-row barleys that are beginning to make a comeback in today's landscape. We also know of flax in these early plots, and of a whole range of other plants which might be described as 'weeds'.

Opportunists in a changing environment
Mixed with the charred cereals in deposits of this period are the round seeds of cleavers and vetch, the small triangular seeds of black bindweed, dock, and knotgrass, the long spindly seeds of brome grass and wild oats, the disc-shaped seeds of fathen and chickweed, and various others besides. These are the plants that have taken advantage of the new

environments of agriculture, and spread from sometimes restricted niches to become common plants.

Some will have travelled across from the Near Eastern steppe together with the cereals. This may be true of wild oats and some of the vetches; others, such as cleavers, invaded from the woodland margins along the route. Fathen and knotgrass probably spread from unstable margins of the rivers that ran beside the early agricultural plots.

An interesting point about the seeds found mixed in with early cereals is their food value. Many are known to have been eaten in various parts of the world in more recent times, and it may be that the same was true in prehistory. Rather than seeing these weeds as something depleting their yields, they may well have been regarded by the farmers as yet another range of resources in their new ecological pyramid.

It is certainly the case that the early farmers did not suffer from a restricted diet. In addition to domestic animals, crops and possibly weeds, they continued to gather acorns, blackberries, barberries, sloes, crab-apples, haws and hazelnuts, and to hunt deer and aurochs for many centuries after the advent of agriculture.

THE EMERGENCE OF MONUMENTAL LANDSCAPES

In addition to all the plants and animals we can place along the river banks, another major feature of the patchwork landscape we have been reconstructing was, of course, the very monument that had incidentally preserved so much of the evidence. In this feature we see a distinct departure from earlier human landscapes. For the first time, human involvement with the environment was extending beyond the purely biological; the topography of the land surface was being artificially modified, sometimes on a substantial scale.

In the two millennia that followed the Elm Decline, such amendment proceeded apace, and the landscape became framed within countless monuments of earth and stone. The legacy of this period still dominates certain areas of our landscape, including the area around the particular barrow we have been examining in detail.

The South Street Long Barrow lies on the outskirts of Avebury, a village that nestles in the upper reaches of the Kennet river in Wiltshire. The river arises 10km (6¼ miles) west of Marlborough from two streams emerging from either side of the chalk downland crest known as Windmill Hill. At the eastern part of the hill's summit the traces of a series of embanked enclosures created over 5000 years ago are still visible. Nearby are a group of round barrows that belong to a later millennium, and on the lower slopes are the worn down remains of the Horslip long barrow, constructed at about the time of the Elm Decline.

The two streams join at the village of Avebury, which nestles within one of the largest monuments in the region. Around 4000 years ago, hundreds of sarsen stones were dragged from the neighbouring valleys, arranged in geometrical patterns, and enclosed within an enormous ditch and bank.

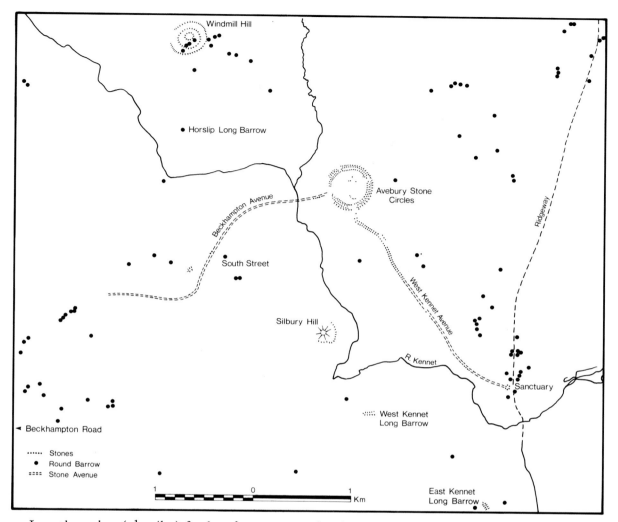

Windmill Hill

Horslip Long Barrow

Beckhampton Avenue

Avebury Stone
Circles

Ridgeway

South Street

West Kennet Avenue

Silbury Hill

R. Kennet

Sanctuary

Beckhampton Road

West Kennet
Long Barrow

······ Stones
• Round Barrow
==== Stone Avenue

1 ___ 0 ___ 1 Km

East Kennet
Long Barrow

Figure 15 Prehistoric sites around Avebury.

Less than 2km (1¼ miles) further downstream, the river passes the enormous grassy cone of Silbury Hill (*Plate 5*) – the largest artificial earthen mound in Europe, the size of the smallest of the Giza pyramids in Egypt. It then runs below a hillslope capped by West Kennet Long Barrow, the largest of its kind in England and Wales, and then, after a further kilometre, the river passes near to the site of a circle of timber and stone fancifully known as the 'Sanctuary', itself linked to the Avebury circle by an 'avenue' of large sarsen stones that stretched for 1.5km (1 mile) across the landscape. Beyond the Sanctuary, an avenue of a different kind can be seen. A series of round barrows cluster along the Ridgeway – a track that has had several millennia of use.

The surprising thing about this artificial landscape is not that farming populations were gradually reaching the sizes necessary for the erection of large monuments, but that none of those monuments seems to have much to do with what we would regard as the mundane aspects of daily life. Living accommodation is extremely elusive, and even the enclosure on Windmill Hill does not seem to have been heavily settled. In fact the range of monuments that came to dominate early agricultural landscapes provide far less evidence of the living than they do of those who had already died.

Landscapes of the dead

Several of the monuments described above actually contain human remains. A notable example is the West Kennet Long Barrow, erected around the time of the Elm Decline, and to which the dead of successive generations were brought for over 1000 years. It is a site that has fascinated antiquaries for centuries, and, by the time it had been subjected to modern excavation techniques, many of the human bones within it were already gone.

A seventeenth-century Dr Toope of Marlborough had shown a particular interest in specimens he noticed being dug up by workmen:

> I quickly perceived they were humane, and came next day and dugg for them, and stored myselfe with many bushells, of which I made a noble medicine that relieved many of my distressed neighbours.

Two centuries later the barrow's contents attracted the attention of Dr John Thurnam of Devizes. His interest was in measuring rather than consuming the bones, in the belief that the racial characteristics of England's earlier inhabitants could be so determined. He was among the foremost figures in this Victorian passion for skull measurement, but less noted for his excavation techniques. West Kennet was one of around 100 barrows he dug into with the aid of the inmates of the Wiltshire County Asylum, of which he was superintendent. It seems they excavated a large part of the monument without an equivalent legacy to archaeological knowledge.

Even with a history such as this the bones of at least 46 humans were still in place by the time the barrow was excavated using modern methods. The actual number is hard to assess, as the bones were not found as complete skeletons. Instead, the stone chambers within the barrow contained a row of skulls in one part, groups of long bones in another, and elsewhere a dump of vertebrae. Finger and toe bones were found in crevices in the stone walls of the chambers, and some had been inserted within the eye sockets of the skulls. Quite clearly, the contemporary community was doing more than simply depositing their dead within such monuments. The bodies were still being handled long after the sinews and tendons had begun to rot.

This handling may have been linked with movement of the bones from the nearby enclosure on the top of Windmill Hill. The ditches of this 'causewayed enclosure', so named on account of the flat areas or causeways that perforate the enclosing ditch, also contained scattered human bones, and this is a feature found on other causewayed enclosures in England. At the Dorset site of Hambledon Hill, Roger Mercer found enough human skeletal debris to suggest:

BURY & SILBURY.   3. 6. 34.   4.113

that the main causewayed enclosure at Hambledon was a vast reeking open cemetery, its silence broken only by the din of crows and ravens.

The same ditches that contain human skeletal fragments often retain considerable evidence of consumption. At Windmill Hill, meat bones are piled up within them, and pottery, flint and charred plant tissue can be found in abundance. A comparison has been drawn with the practices of a group of Indians who inhabited southern Ontario in Canada.

Up until the end of the seventeenth century, the Huron Indians held, at intervals, a feast of the dead. Every ten years or so the recently deceased were disinterred in preparation for this feast. The relatively intact bodies were carried whole to the place of the feast, and the less intact cleaned up and wrapped in beaver skins. The motley collection of bodies and bundles was assembled on scaffolding around a large pit

Plate 5 Aerial view looking southwards across Avebury Circle towards Silbury Hill. On the hillslopes beyond, West Kennet Long Barrow is situated (photo: Major G. Allen).

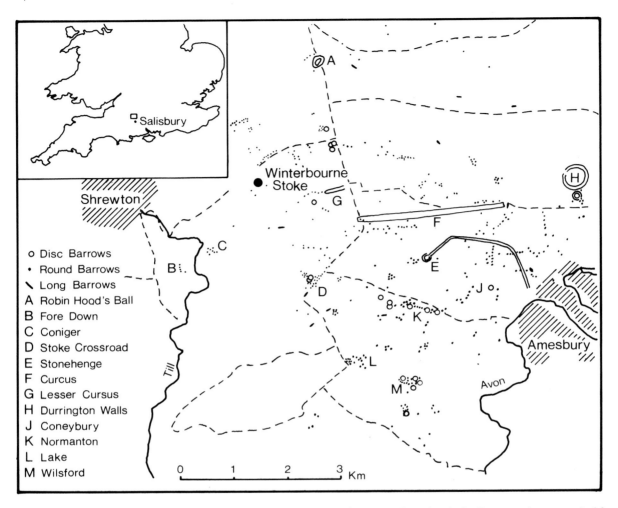

Figure 16 Prehistoric sites around Stonehenge.

within which they were subsequently reburied. Ceremonies were held and gifts were given; the feast of the dead was an opportunity to re-emphasise wealth, alliance and power. In addition to a display of the gifts brought by each village and clan group, the master of ceremonies made a formal announcement of each series of gifts, for all to hear and no doubt to compare.

Patterns in the broader landscape

Whatever rituals surrounded the disposal of the dead in the centuries that followed the Elm Decline, we can be certain of one thing: those who toiled in early agricultural clearings would have seen the landscape as a source of sustenance, as being closely intertwined with the landscape as the realm of the ancestors. It could hardly be otherwise, for the monuments to the dead were not confined to special enclosures like our modern cemeteries, but were spread widely in the landscape, and the cultivation of soil and grazing of herds took place right alongside them.

Through time the burial rites changed: the bodies were treated in different ways and placed within different structures. Yet the prominence within the landscape of monuments to the dead remained. It is as if the landscape was marked out by these monuments; as though a farmer, on looking up from his toil, would be reminded by the massive barrows on the horizon of ancestral rights over the land he was working. It is perhaps for this reason that so many barrows were sited such that they had maximum visibility from afar.

Yet not everywhere were such monuments easily visible. The archaeological landscape of the fourth and third millennia BC is not made up of structures that are evenly distributed across the countryside; there are dense clusters of monuments, as in the Upper Kennet Valley, and, conversely, there are areas in which monuments are sparse. This patterning across large areas in itself provides clues about the way these landscapes were organised.

In a radius of 5km (3 miles) around Avebury village, at least eight long barrows and a causewayed enclosure had been constructed by about the end of the fourth millennium BC. By the second millennium BC, Silbury Hill and Avebury circle had been erected along with two stone avenues, a further stone circle and the Sanctuary, and in the region of 100 round barrows.

Yet a few kilometres further south of Avebury, in the Vale of Pewsey, the density of barrows falls off to less than two per square kilometre, and other monuments of the period are similarly sparse. Further south still, these monuments once again become prolific.

In this next concentration, 25km (15½ miles) to the south of Avebury, we know of some ten long barrows and a causewayed enclosure, two 'cursus' monuments, approximately 400 round barrows, and four 'henge' monuments, including the best known of them all, Stonehenge.

Many of today's visitors to Stonehenge and Avebury, while admiring the stones themselves, remain oblivious to the vast numbers of funerary and ritual monuments within a few hours' walk. For several centuries, even though custom and ritual changed, it was these same nuclei within the landscape that were marked out by different generations of monument.

If we look further afield, it seems that this regional clustering of monuments is a repeated phenomenon. In addition, it seems normal for the same pattern of clustering to be maintained for several centuries.

To the south of Stonehenge, there is another cluster along Cranbourne Chase. Here we find the massive Dorset Cursus, a linear enclosure running for almost 10km (6¼ miles), and nearby, the causewayed enclosure at Hambledon Hill. Long barrows and round barrows are concentrated in the vicinity, and to the south-east in the parish of Knowlton lie two henge monuments (*Plate 6*). Within one of these henges sits a small church, a reminder of the continued spiritual reinterpretation over the millennia of these enigmatic legacies of distant generations.

We can follow this pattern of monument clusters south, to the nucleus

Figure 17 Barrow clusters
and associated monuments in
central southern England
(adapted from R. Bradley
and A. Ellison 1975 *Ram's
Hill*).

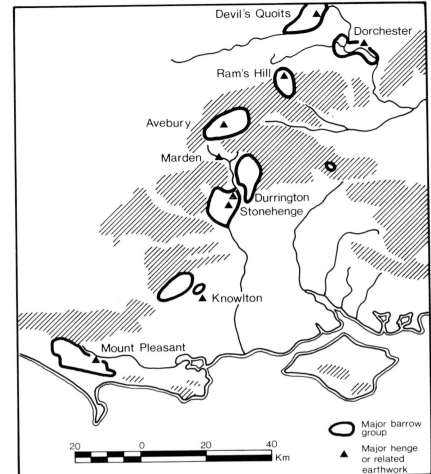

along the Dorset ridgeway, and north, to further nuclei within the
Upper Thames Valley, the Chilterns, the East Anglian fen edge, the
Mendips, the Peak District, the Yorkshire Wolds, the North York
Moors, and no doubt many other places besides.

If the control over the agricultural landscape was linked to these
prominent monuments, then the land between these clusters could well
have remained as wildwood. We find isolated barrows within these
peripheral areas, perhaps where a thinner population collected to
acknowledge their immediate ancestors. While such scattered
populations might remain most of the time in relative isolation, farming
small plots and making extensive use of woodland resources, they would
have on occasion to make the journey upstream to the land of their
distant ancestors.

Here a much larger lineage group would collect to exchange goods
and gossip, and to seek out potential spouses. They might have to pay
dues to a 'protective' core group, whose power was vested in their

Plate 6 Knowlton Henge, Dorset. A ruined church sits within the henge from which it is separated by over 3000 years. A second, much larger henge monument survives, partly as a cropmark, and partly as an earthwork covered by the trees that surround the modern farm. In the near vicinity are the remains of countless other prehistoric sites (photo: RCHME).

control of the major funerary rituals, and in the knowledge that people had gathered to these same nuclei within the landscape for centuries.

Knowledge and power

We can see many ways in which a core group within society might have marked itself off from the rest by displaying its superior knowledge and power. The knowledge that is most evident from the monuments that remain is of surveying and geometry, and of the pattern of celestial events.

An archaeological map of the Stonehenge environs well illustrates the level of understanding of surveying and geometry that was being invested in the marking out of the landscape by the second millennium BC. Stonehenge itself is made up of a series of concentric circles, of which only the innermost ones are marked by lintel-bearing sarsens. Connecting these concentric circles with the river Avon is a ditch and bank 'avenue', which follows a topographic course for most of its course, but for the final stretch towards the monument follows a dead straight line.

The imposition of straight lines can be seen elsewhere in the environs of the monument. Less than 1 km ($\frac{5}{8}$ mile) to the north, an extended ditch and bank rectangle follows a straight course for almost 3 km (1$\frac{3}{4}$ miles).

This is one of the cursus monuments, the longest of which, extending for nearly 10km (6¼ miles), is the Dorset Cursus mentioned above. Both the Dorset and the Stonehenge cursus monuments adopt a perpendicular alignment from a pre-existing long barrow and are respected by subsequent round barrows. Following a south-west alignment from near to the west end of the Stonehenge cursus lies a series of round barrows, arranged more or less along a straight line, and running up to a pre-existing long barrow. Several linear barrow cemeteries of this kind may be found in the near vicinity.

The Stonehenge region is one of the more spectacular examples of the geometry that had been imposed on the landscape in the millennia that followed the Elm Decline. But the regular patterns created by stone circles, stone rows, cursus, and linear barrow cemeteries are widespread, and occur throughout Britain and in parts of northern France. A great deal of interest has been shown in the fine detail of their geometry by Alexander Thom and others, and also in their relationship with the geometry of the heavens. Again we can return to Stonehenge as an example.

Some have argued that Stonehenge served as an observatory of solar and lunar events, and the positioning of the stones in relation to the rising of the midsummer sun is well known. It has also been argued that, at exactly right angles to this alignment, the monument marks the rising of the midsummer moon. In order to create such a pattern, the site of Stonehenge had to be carefully selected. A few kilometres one way or another and the pattern would be lost. Observations spanning several years may have gone into the original siting of the monument in order to create this pattern. Other solar and lunar events predicted may have formed the basis of a ceremonial calendar, much as the complex Aztec calendar of the New World fixed ceremonial events within a 52-year cycle.

There should be nothing surprising about a society remote from ourselves having a detailed knowledge of the heavens. It is common for both hunter-gatherer and pre-industrial farming communities to organise their food-gathering cycles, migratory movements and seasonal rituals around the stars. It is only the minority of cultures whose knowledge of the heavens is restricted to the most obvious features, and even they will be familiar with such features as the Pleiades, the belt of Orion and the planet Venus.

What is more notable about the societies that created the geometric landscapes of British prehistory, is that this knowledge of the heavens, gathered over generations, was translated into massive structures that reflect the mobilisation of immense quantities of manpower.

Power, scale, and the end of the landscape of ancestors
We see then by the second millennium BC the appearance of cultivated landscapes that were consciously and profoundly structured by their occupants, linked through time with their ancestral inhabitants, and through space with the geometry of the land surface and the heavens.

The understanding of the pattern of these links could have rested with a core group who used that knowledge to exercise power over the people who gathered around the monuments, and who caused them to embellish the landscape with ever greater monuments for subsequent gatherings.

Many of the monuments mentioned in this chapter are of a substantial size, and their erection must have involved the coordinated efforts of large numbers of people. By quantifying the earth, stone and timber involved, the distance it needed to move and the work involved in its preparation, we can gain a rough measure of the overall effort the erection of each monument entailed.

The earlier monuments suggest control of manpower on a fairly restricted scale. The causewayed enclosures, which may have formed the focus of communal feasting, exchange and celebration of the dead, and the contemporary long barrows in the adjacent landscape, could each have been erected by small groups of families, collectively investing between 10,000 and 50,000 man-hours in each monument.

By the time henges appeared, monuments were being constructed on a much greater scale; there are several henge monuments that could have absorbed 300,000 to 500,000 man-hours. The control of manpower had shifted to a different level in which more than a few families were involved.

One monument in this category is Stonehenge itself. Its construction can be divided up into three broad phases, of which the second phase could have been achieved with around 360,000 man-hours of work. This is the stage before the massive trilithons were erected; they did not appear until late in the day of landscapes dominated by monuments of earth and stone. By the time the last stones were put in place, the construction of henge monuments and stone circles elsewhere had long since ceased, and the creation of new barrows was giving way to the re-use of existing sites for cremation burials.

Estimates of the manpower involved in the construction of this final, extravagant phase in the life of the best known monument of the period vary between two and 30 million man-hours. Despite its impressive scale, the final rebuild of Stonehenge comes towards the twilight of that long epoch in which the agricultural landscape was organised and controlled around strange, geometrical monuments that linked the earth with the heavens and the living with the dead.

The human landscapes that were created in its place would never again present so enigmatic a legacy to our modern imaginations; their stones and barrows remain to puzzle and intrigue us. Whatever the reason for the demise of their world, the one that superseded it was organised in a manner more compatible with our own world-view. In place of patterns created by earthen mounds and massive stones, the new landscapes were framed within field-walls and boundaries that were clearly visible on the ground. In the second millennium BC we see the emergence of more 'modern', familiar landscapes, and it is to these landscapes that we now turn.

5

Field-boundaries and frontiers

We have seen how the monuments of earth and stone that proliferated across England's early agricultural landscapes illuminate two separate aspects of the contemporary environment. On the one hand, their prominent forms above ground could be related to the human inhabitants of that environment, not just their beliefs and their social organisation, but also the way they mobilised their manpower resources. On the other hand, the land surfaces buried beneath the monuments provide evidence of the land they inhabited, the soils they tilled and how these soils had responded to agricultural use.

In the new ecological pyramid that farming communities had created, these two themes, manpower and land, were crucial elements in the equation of human survival and population growth. As numbers grew, so could effort be invested in diverting ever more of the ecosystem towards the sustenance of humans, placing ever greater demands on the soil.

The monuments quite incidentally plot this process through time. On the one hand they reflect how the scales of manpower coordinated in their construction increased, from the family groups that erected long barrows to the vast numbers engaged in the final rebuild of Stonehenge. On the other hand, the land surfaces buried beneath those monuments reflect a concomitant decline in soil quality. The soils beneath the banks of some of the henge monuments show signs of being leached, and several round barrows overlie soils that have become starved of nutrients.

This process of soil deterioration we shall examine in detail in a later chapter. At this stage we can simply observe that, as the numbers of people involved in monument building increased, so it seems that the stress on the soils they tilled and grazed gradually took its toll. This in turn may be connected with the dramatic change in the landscape that occurred during the course of the second millennium BC.

It is during this period that, for the first time, vast tracts of land were enclosed within tangible, visible field-boundaries and frontiers. The enclosure of a plot of land within a distinct boundary implies that land is at a premium, a concept so familiar to us that we tend to treat it as a universal truth. It is easy to forget that when the human population was much more sparsely distributed, manpower rather than land was at a premium and the forging of cooperative relationships between people

Figure 18 Map of locations cited in Chapter 5.

was more critical to survival than the acquisition of land. Indeed this may be exactly what we are seeing in the conspicuous control of manpower discussed in the previous chapter. If this were the case, the changes that took place in the second millennium BC would correspond to a shift from manpower to land as the limiting factor in human survival.

The transition towards enclosed prehistoric landscapes has left copious traces in the modern landscape, and analyses of them have allowed us to understand some aspects of that transition. A prime example is the work that has been done on the granite mass of Dartmoor in Devon, where such traces are exceptionally well preserved.

THE DARTMOOR REEVES

There is a well-worn track across part of Dartmoor that connects the small settlements of Huccaby, Combestone and Dartmeet with Widecombe-on-the-Moor. Along its length may be found landmarks of its usage in previous centuries. A simple dry stone 'clapper bridge' spans the river Dart, and nearby is the 'coffin stone' that marks the coffin bearers' weary route, at a time when the dead of Dartmeet had to be carried across 8km (5 miles) of rugged moor to the nearest graveyard at Widecombe. These relics are, however, among the more recent landmarks along the track.

Two kilometres ($1\frac{1}{4}$ miles) outside Widecombe, the purple heather blanketing the moor is punctuated by a series of slight ridges. These ridges, or 'reeves' as they are locally known, are long, relatively straight structures, composed in this instance of small stones, piled up to about 0.5m (20in) high and about three times the width, and overgrown with heather and moss.

Along this track from Widecombe to Dartmeet, the reeves remain in view running alongside the track and more or less parallel to it, at a spacing of about 800m (2625ft). As the path crosses the Eastern Dart river, heather moor gives way to farmland, but the line of the reeves is still to be seen. Indeed, the modern fields visible on the river's western bank are divided by walls and hedges that seem to echo the same pattern of long parallel divisions. A kilometre ($\frac{5}{8}$ mile) further on, the track descends into the hamlet of Sherwell, and from here the reeve system comes fully and strikingly into view.

A whole series of these linear structures stretches out in front of the path, filling the visible landscape with its ordered pattern. The view ahead is studded with steep, rock-capped tors and sharply dissected valleys. Yet the reeves run straight ahead, unperturbed by this uneven topography. They run high among the granite boulders and bare ground that crown the tors. From here they descend into the heather and grass, never deviating from their course.

Some 20 or so reeves follow this route across the tors and down to the river Dart. On a clear day the same reeves can be made out in the far distance, towards their limits on the slopes of Holne Moor (*Plate 7*). This

particular system of reeves encompasses an area of 32 sq. km (12¼ sq. miles), and it is only one of several such systems on Dartmoor.

As early as 1825, these reeves were described as 'ancient dykes or division lines', and a number of Victorian antiquaries believed them to be prehistoric. Their existence was neglected by many archaeologists of this century, and it is only in recent years that Andrew Fleming and others have placed their construction securely within the second millennium BC (*Plates 8 and 9*).

The kind of evidence used to establish a date is not from the reeves themselves, but from structures intimately associated with them. For example, towards the southern end of the Dartmeet system on Holne Moor, some other structures may be seen within the reeves – the stubby remains of stone-built round houses, surviving only as a circle of

Plate 7 Aerial view of the Dartmeet system of reeves on Holne Moor (photo: Naval Air Squadron).

misshapen stones. In places they are structurally linked to the reeves themselves, reflecting their contemporaneity.

A number of these round houses, which are found right across the moor, have been excavated, and a certain amount of pottery has been retrieved from them. This pottery, and the carbon dates that exist for a few of the sites, places the houses and the associated reeves securely within the second millennium BC. In these reeves, therefore, we are clearly looking at a form of landscape that followed immediately on from the landscape of ancestors.

Plate 9 The Venford Reeve during excavation (photo: A. Fleming).

In many places we can trace the development from one form of landscape to the other. Dartmoor has its share of burial mounds, and several are incorporated into later reeve systems, in a way that suggests continuity of land division, marked out in different ways in different centuries.

Just as Wessex has its linear cursus and stone avenues, so Dartmoor has its single, double or treble stone rows. These too are in some cases clearly respected by the later reeves, though in others their significance has obviously been ignored or forgotten.

The Dartmoor Reeve Project

Since 1975, Sheffield University and the Central Excavation Unit have been undertaking a programme of research into the origin and development of the reeve systems on Dartmoor, drawing on modern methods of excavation, landscape archaeology and environmental archaeology. One aspect of the project has been a survey of the moor, both on foot and from the air, and by combing all the records and references to these structures that have accrued over the years. Alongside this survey, two parts of the reeve system have been excavated: on Shaugh Moor in the valley of the River Plym, that drains from the south-west of Dartmoor, and on Holne Moor in the valley of the river Dart, draining from the east. In conjunction with these

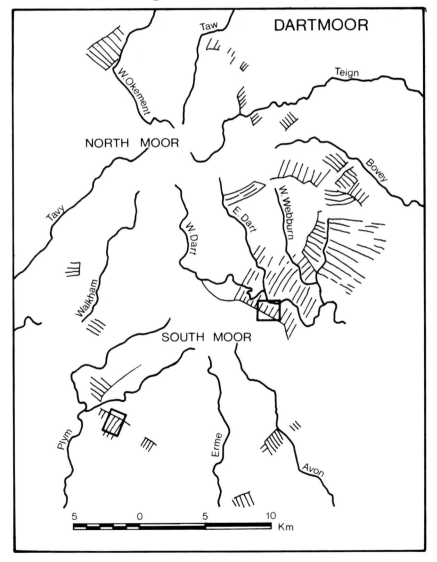

Figure 19 Parallel systems on Dartmoor, showing locations of areas depicted in Figures 20 and 21.

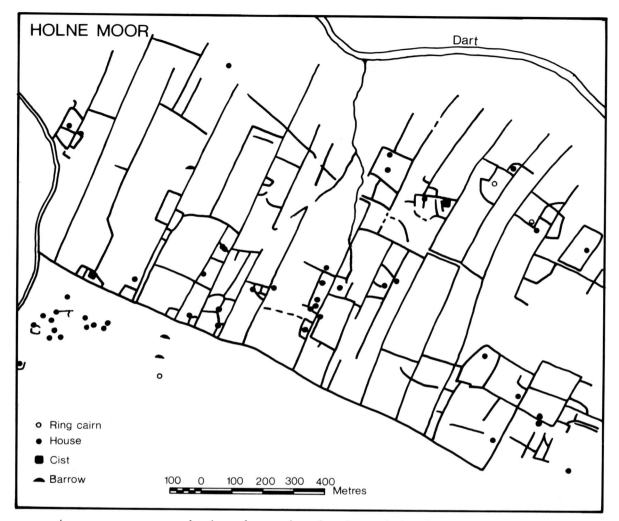

HOLNE MOOR

Dart

o Ring cairn
• House
■ Cist
▲ Barrow

100 0 100 200 300 400
Metres

excavations, numerous samples have been taken for the analysis of biological remains of the contemporary landscape.

The detailed survey has greatly increased the extent of our knowledge of reeves. In addition to the ones that are clearly visible, such as those encountered between Widecombe and Dartmeet, much slighter examples have been found that are only visible with a light covering of snow. Air survey has extended the pattern further still. Andrew Fleming, who has led the survey, is now able to distinguish ten separate territories among the reeve systems of Dartmoor, and to say something about the characteristics of each system.

They vary in area between less than 200 and more than 3000ha (494 to 7413 acres), and each territory may be internally divided into two or three zones. They are divided first between low moor and high moor by a reeve running along the contours between 350m (1148ft) and 400m (1312ft) above sea level. This could well be a division that was, prior to

Figure 20 Parallel system on Holne Moor, Dartmoor (after A. Fleming).

Figure 21 Parallel system on Shaugh Moor, Dartmoor (after G. Wainwright).

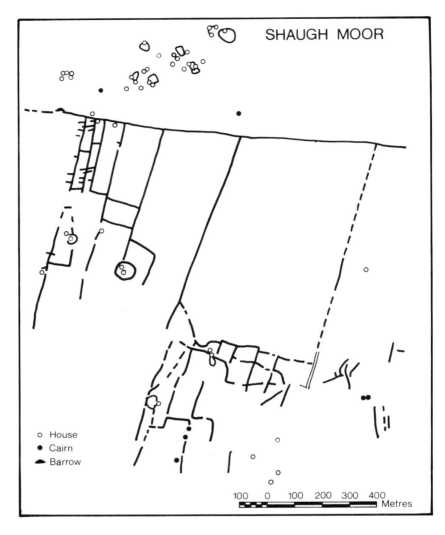

reeve building, demarcated by funerary cairns and stone rows, monuments which are often found just above this line. On the high moor above this contour reeve, the absence of further subdivisions might suggest common access. Below lies an area of parallel reeves joining the contour reeve at right angles to it. In the general vicinity of this boundary, round houses cluster into 'neighbourhood groups', usually in conjunction with smaller enclosures and paddocks.

In the southern part of Dartmoor we can add a third zone, of dispersed settlement along river valleys, perhaps reflecting seasonal upland grazing of a type of valley-slope pasture only encountered in the south of the moor.

In addition to examining the spatial organisation of the reeves, the project has used the methods of excavation to probe back through time to explore their origins.

The origin of the Dartmoor reeves

The landscape into which the reeves were placed had already been subject to millennia of human interference. The wildwood that covered the lower slopes of the moor had been cleared and exploited both by hunter-gatherer and farming communities, who left their impression both in pollen diagrams and as scatters of flint. By the time the first reeves were laid out, much of the landscape had become scrubby grassland, maintained by the grazing of domestic flocks and herds.

In examining the creation of reeve systems within this landscape, we can draw a contrast between their conception and their execution. Each system was conceived within a single plan; this much is clear from their ordered pattern. Bearing in mind how some of the neighbouring systems interlock with one another, there is even an argument that co-ordinated planning extended beyond the individual territory.

Yet their execution was piecemeal; short stretches of a single reeve were constructed in entirely different ways. A single reeve might change its form of construction along its length a number of times, incorporating various combinations of ditches, banks, wooden fences, and perhaps hedges.

These earliest reeves predate the stone ones we see today. On both Shaugh Moor and Holne Moor, the stone reeves overlie earlier structures of earth and wood. These can be found by excavating beneath the existing reeves; where the ground is waterlogged, the excavators have even been able to unearth the oak stakes of the earlier fences that were ripped out to make way for the later, more durable boundaries.

At some stage the motley collection of ditches, banks and barriers of wood dividing up the Dartmoor landscape gave way to the partitions of stone we see today, and at the same time, wooden round houses are replaced by houses of stone. The stone reeves were no more uniform than their predecessors. Once again, there is a contrast between the co-ordinated plan and the piecemeal execution. In places the new reeves were formed from simple piles of small boulders, forming a broad enough base to bear a turf superstructure. Elsewhere such piles are interrupted at intervals by stone uprights, about a metre in height, and we can presume the gaps between these uprights were filled, again with something like turf. In other places, the reeves are faced on both sides with large slabs. As with the earlier reeves, the impression is of separate small groups of builders, using different styles, but working within a common grand plan.

The reeves in an ecological context

To explore the way in which these planned landscapes were used we can turn to the pollen evidence from the Shaugh Moor area. Peat cores were taken from four separate locations within 4km ($2\frac{1}{2}$ miles) of one another, running from within the Shaugh Moor parallel reeve system itself, up out onto the high moor beyond the contour reeve.

The general picture derived from these cores for the second millennium BC is of rough pasture with patches of scrub. Common among the pasture were sedges, cinquefoil, plantain and ferns, and sheep's sorrel, devil's bit scabious, and several members of the dandelion family could have been found. The scrubby patches contained oak, birch, hazel and dog-rose. Alder carr colonised the wetter places, and heathland was spreading around the Blacka Brook, a stream to the north of the contour reeve.

The ratio between grassland and scrub pollen varies between sampling points. The core from within the parallel reeve system, at Wotter Common, has more grassland weeds and less woodland than any of the other cores, and it is only here that we find evidence for cereal cultivation. It seems that cultivated plants were not a major feature of these early Dartmoor landscapes, and wheat, barley and beans would have been brought in from lower, more sheltered areas. That they were brought in is clear not only from the traces of their seeds and pollen, but also from the numerous cereal grinding stones recovered from excavations at Shaugh Moor.

Moving from the vegetation cover to the animals that grazed upon it, an unfortunate corollary of the high soil acidity that preserves pollen so well is that animal bones rarely survive. We can, however, track down the livestock that grazed in the rough pasture in a more unusual way.

Careful excavation of the ditches that in places marked out the reeve boundaries on Shaugh Moor uncovered a mass of ancient animal footprints. These boundary lines were clearly heavily exposed to animal traffic that was being herded along the border ditches and kept from straying into the neighbouring plots, a reminder of the land rights these new boundaries delineated.

From these impressions at Shaugh Moor we gain a very clear picture of the steady movement of herds of cattle and flocks of sheep, their countless footprints merging into a wet messy slurry. The occasional print of a horse hoof perhaps relates to a prehistoric cowboy controlling the movement. A badger print reminds us of the wild animals in the landscape.

Against this broad background of the second millennium BC environment, we can examine more closely how the advent of reeves relates to this picture. To do this, we must turn from the pollen in the peat to the pollen in the soils buried by reeve construction. By looking at five sample points along two of the reeves, the soil pollen could be matched with that from a nearby peat core, and the reeve construction thus placed within the sequence derived from that core.

This soil pollen suggests that while the extent of grazing, and therefore the extent of wooded cover, fluctuated through time, the predominant use of the landscape both before and after the construction of the reeves was rough grazing. So the creation of these land divisions seems not to have involved a dramatic change in land use. The change was in the control over land, not what was done with it.

Environmental and landscape archaeology at Dartmoor have thus allowed us to place the transition from a landscape of cairns and stone rows to one divided up by parallel reeves into some sort of context. We can see that the transition does not occur at a time of massive change in the living landscape; before and after the construction of the reeves, the environment on the moors is one of rough grazed pasture.

Within this rough pasture, however, there are signs that the soils were deteriorating and the heath was spreading. This may have been a crucial factor in the increasing concern with access to the diminishing returns from the overworked soil, and subsequent moves towards land enclosure.

Working within a grand scheme of land allotment, individual families put up fences and dug ditches to demarcate what was theirs. This system of allotment was rooted in the much older land rights linked to the funerary monuments, but in places these older rights had already been forgotten. Livestock had to be contained within these newly allotted areas, and access to the common grazing lands of the high moor was along the boundaries of intervening plots, where we can still see their clustered footprints.

The Dartmoor evidence is unusual in terms of the extent of the evidence that has been gathered from it, but it is by no means unique. The reeves constitute but a single example of the parallel systems of land boundaries that became widespread during the second millennium BC.

PARALLEL SYSTEMS BEYOND DARTMOOR

The Dartmoor reeves are among the earlier forms of parallel land division, but they are not the earliest. To find these we must go beyond England to western Ireland. Here boundaries similar to the Dartmoor reeves are common, not on the surface, but beneath the blanket peat.

Between Behy and Glenulra on the coast of County Mayo, a series of such parallel reeves runs up to the modern cliff edge. It is visible towards the cliffs, but inland is smothered by peat bog. Carbon dating has shown that this bog started growing in the late third millennium BC, and so the reeve system it smothers must be older still.

The earliest known parallel systems in England appear somewhere between the late third and early second millennia BC. One of these is the series of enclosures at Fengate on the East Anglian fen edge. This group is made up of rectangular paddocks interlocking with droveways that link the fens themselves with the higher, drier fen edge. The excavator, Francis Pryor, envisages the seasonal migration of farmer and stock along hedge-lined droveways, from the drier land to the fen pasture below, in a manner that reminds us of the hoofprints along the reeve edge leading up to the high moor on Dartmoor.

As the second millennium progressed, parallel reeve-like systems were to appear in many parts of the British Isles. Numerous examples may be cited from England alone. In the south and east such systems are known in Wessex and Sussex, and in the west around Bristol and Somerset, Cornwall and the Scilly Isles. To the north there is a massive system stretching out along the Bunter Sandstone in Nottinghamshire and Yorkshire, and a smaller system in Swaledale in North Yorkshire.

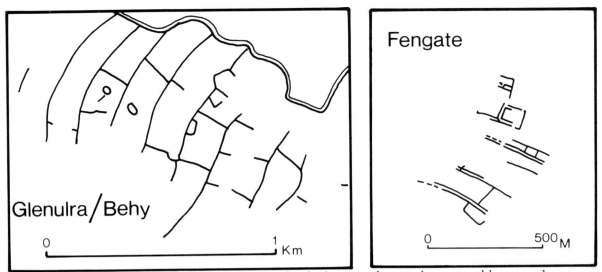

Fengate

0   1
⌐   ⌐ Km

0   500 M

Figure 22 Early parallel systems of land division. *Left*: Glenulra/Behy, County Mayo (after S. Caulfield); *right*: Fengate, Peterborough (after F. Pryor).

In the stony uplands they may bear a close resemblance to the reeves of Dartmoor. Elsewhere they take on different forms. Such is the case on the Berkshire Downs, to the south-east of Wantage. This area of downland is fertile, green and relatively stone-free. It is now largely under the plough, and although no reeve-like structures can be seen, at certain times of year, and in certain lights, a series of parallel shadows can be discerned across the tops of the growing corn. From the air these cropmarks crystalise into a complex pattern of land-divisions organised into blocks often of several square kilometres in extent.

There are certain similarities between the Dartmoor reeves and the Berkshire Downs examples, beyond their common parallel structure and similar scale. Just as it is common for the funerary monuments on Dartmoor to either lie a little beyond the reeves in open land, or to be incorporated into the reeve boundaries themselves, so on the Berkshire Downs a dense cluster of barrows known as the Lambourn group remains unenclosed, and some of the outliers of this group are incorporated into the land divisions on either side.

We can see then a number of points of similarity in the early development of these various systems of enclosure, their parallel structure, their frequent relationship with the preceding funerary landscape, and an occasional hint of the droving of animals to an adjacent area of common grazing. Through time those forms of those enclosed landscapes develop and change, but in different ways in different places.

The development of parallel systems through time

In subsequent periods, the Dartmoor reeves remained relatively intact. Subdivisions and cross walls appear in many places, but the dominant parallel structure has persisted through to the present day. This may be a function of Dartmoor's declining population in subsequent millennia. As the spreading heath lessened the quality of the land, so the human

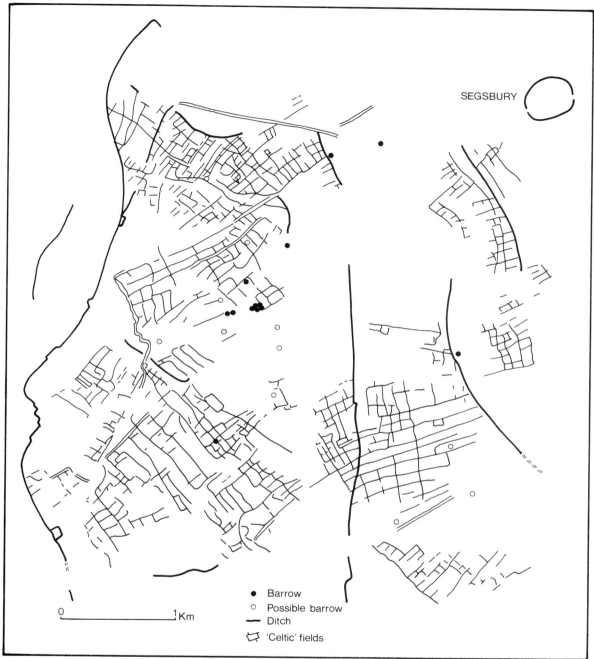

SEGSBURY

● Barrow
○ Possible barrow
— Ditch
⬦ 'Celtic' fields

0 _____ 1 Km

population thinned, and the early land divisions became to some extent fossilised.

This is not the case with the chalklands of southern Britain; through time the enclosures were modified on several occasions. The parallel system on Bockhampton Down is criss-crossed with a chequerboard of

Figure 23 Prehistoric boundaries near Segsbury on the Berkshire Downs (adapted from J. Richards 1978 *The archaeology of the Berkshire Downs*).

later subdivisions, in some places so densely packed that the original parallel skeleton is obscured. These subdivisions are examples of the so-called 'Celtic fields', well known on the chalk, and often visible from the ground as lynchets. In Chapter 1 we encountered one such set at Fyfield Down near Avebury.

At a subsequent stage, this mass of subdivisions was loosely framed within boundaries of a rather different kind. Long, sinous, and often substantial ditches stretched across the landscape, dividing it up into units that may be the size of modern parishes, or even larger.

THE ENCLOSURE OF LARGER UNITS

A number of such boundaries along the Berkshire Downs can be discerned from the air, and here and there stretches of those boundaries survive as quite substantial earthworks. These long sinuous boundaries have sometimes been called 'ranch boundaries', suggesting a function related to stock management. We have seen, however, that prehistoric boundaries may have more to do with rights over land than with what went on within them, and indeed the land they contained may have served many different purposes in the long history of their use.

On Bockhampton Down and the neighbouring parts of the Berkshire Downs, these ditches run down perpendicularly from the ridge of the Downs across its dip slope, much in the same way as many of the modern parish boundaries. Indeed the ditches at Uffington and Liddington are for part of their length coincident with parish boundaries, and a stretch at East Garton runs parallel to a parish boundary at a distance of 500m (1640ft). The ditch on Uffington Down runs up to an Iron Age hillfort and, like many such boundaries, is aligned on pre-existing round barrows.

We can thus see the link through time between the modern wire fence that lies along the boundary separating the parishes of Woolstone and Uffington, a second millennium BC land division, and a pair of round barrows that may have demarcated that same land division approximately 4000 years earlier than the wire fence.

Just as parallel systems are widespread and extensive, so are these linear ditch boundaries. They divide up much of the Wessex landscape into sinuous blocks of land, and in some cases may be followed as surviving earthworks for several kilometres across the landscape. A very complete system is known around Sidbury and Quarley in Wiltshire and Hampshire.

We can follow these sinuous boundaries westward to the county boundary of Dorset. Leaving this county on the A354, a modest road sign announces the entry into Hampshire. Just beyond the road sign is a much less modest boundary marker in the form of Bokerley Dyke, a massive ditch and bank structure which coincides with the county boundary for 5km (3 miles) of its length. Various excavations have shown that this dyke dates back at least as far as the Roman period, and aerial photography takes it back further still. It can be seen to form the

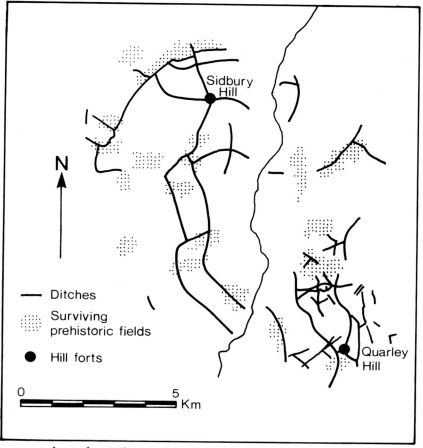

Figure 24 Linear boundaries and areas of prehistoric fields around Sidbury and Quarley (adapted from R. Palmer 1984 *Danebury: an aerial photographic interpretation of its environs* and C. Taylor 1975 *Fields in the English Landscape*).

western boundary of a whole series of sinuous ditches across Wessex, incorporating the Sidbury/Quarley earthworks mentioned above. It appears that this section at least of England's county boundaries was already established as some kind of frontier 3000 to 4000 years ago.

Ancient enclosure and modern enclosure

At first sight, the middle of the country may appear too disrupted by medieval ploughing and parliamentary enclosure to preserve any trace of prehistoric land divisions. Yet it may be that in many cases, as on Dartmoor and Wessex, the ancient land divisions coincide with the modern, and that existing hedges and walls preserve the line of some very ancient boundaries. On the Penwith peninsular in Cornwall (*Plate 10*) the bank of one of the existing hedges was found to contain within its makeup a hoard of prehistoric bronzework. At Great Bourton in Oxfordshire, the boundaries of medieval fields of ridge and furrow can be seen to coincide with the cropmarks of Roman or earlier boundaries. Evidence such as this, and the fact that county and parish boundaries sometimes preserve prehistoric divisions, lead us to ask whether other field boundaries that are still in use preserve much earlier divisions.

Plate 10 Prehistoric field boundaries still in use on the Penwith Peninsular, Cornwall (photo: RCHME).

An interesting case in point is the field systems of East Anglia. In several parishes, the plan of modern field boundaries is very reminiscent of the pattern of reeves, with parallel divisions continuing across the landscape with apparent disregard for other topographical features. Around Tilbury, on the Thames in Essex, a whole series of road and field boundaries follow the lines of an extended parallel system, with a spacing interval very similar to those found on Dartmoor. Small parts of this system have been excavated at Orsett and Mucking, and have been shown to have a pre-medieval date. Close inspection of other modern tracks and hedges will no doubt reveal further hints of reeve-like systems in the agricultural heartlands.

We can contrast these heartlands, in which any original parallel divisions are likely to be engulfed in the complexities of subsequent

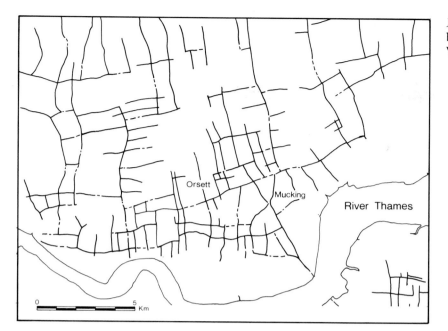

Figure 25 Selected modern boundaries in Essex (after W. Rodwell).

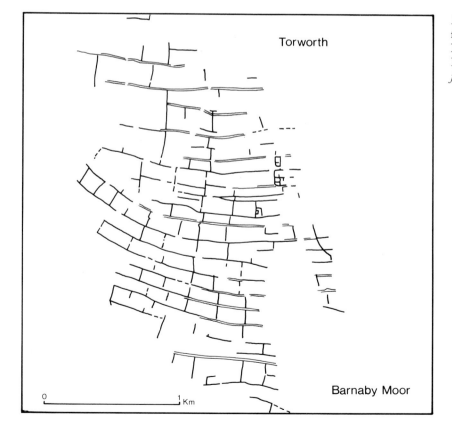

Figure 26 A parallel system from near Worksop, Nottinghamshire (after D. Riley 1980 *Early landscapes from the air*).

phases of enclosure and subdivision, with areas like Dartmoor in which the eventual marginality of the land slowed the process of structural change, leaving much of the reeve system intact. When medieval farmers colonised the moor, they frequently adopted the same land boundaries their predecessors had used centuries earlier.

In the same way a parallel system that spreads over a 50km (31 mile) stretch of the Bunter Sandstone in Nottinghamshire and Yorkshire, which is almost certainly prehistoric in origin, appears to have been re-occupied in the third century AD. Around a scatter of Roman farmsteads seen on aerial photographs, a parallel reeve-like system is clearly discernible.

Settlement within a bounded landscape

During the course of the second millennium BC, we can see in various parts of the English landscape, especially over the southern chalklands, three broad phases of land division. At first a symbolic landscape of the fourth and third millennia BC, marked out by enigmatic monuments and places of the dead was superseded by a series of tangible land boundaries, organised as parallel systems. These parallel systems were in turn subdivided, breaking up the parallel units into a patchwork of Celtic fields. At a later stage still, long, substantial ditches broke up the developing patchwork into much larger units.

As the exploited landscape becomes fixed in this way within permanent boundaries, so we can begin to see a relationship develop with the settlements that grow up within and around them. During the second millennium a number of the known settlements are clearly nested within the surrounded field system, but as the second millennium gives way to the first, two new trends in settlement may be detected.

The first trend is the siting of hillforts at many of the intersections between the long boundary ditches. Examples include the hillforts at Sidbury (*Plate 11*), and Quarley, and many that occur along the crest of the Berkshire Downs. Even where the details of a ditch system are no longer visible, individual fragments of ditch can be seen stretching out from several hillforts.

The second trend involves the piecemeal addition of individual fields onto the body of existing fields. These can be seen clustering around the edges of many large, rectilinear blocks of fields. Their haphazard, lobe-like form contrasts with the organised rectilinear structure of the fields that grew up within the parallel systems, and betrays the much smaller scale on which they were planned.

The two trends thus reflect human behaviour on two different scales. The hillforts, set at nodal points within the enclosed landscape and densely packed with archaeological debris, reflect the coordinated activities of large numbers of people working within the landscape. The new fields, on the other hand, reflect the activities of small groups of farmers, enclosing what may have been common land on an individual basis.

SIDBURY. 28 5 33

The first millennium is also a time when the evidence of human settlement in the English landscape becomes far more plentiful; we are able to focus in much more detail than has hitherto been possible on the range of human activity in the landscape, from the coordinated action of large gatherings of people in hillforts to the actions of individual farmers enclosing small groups of fields. This rich body of data and its implications for the development of the English landscape are explored in the next two chapters.

Plate 11 Sidbury Hill, Wiltshire: beyond the hillfort itself a linear boundary earthwork can be seen, stretching off into the distance (photo: Major G. Allen).

6

Gathering together

The hills that rise between the rivers Iwerne and Stour on Cranbourne Chase in Dorset are capped by two substantial hillforts of the first millennium BC. One is Hambledon Hill, also the site of one of the causewayed enclosures mentioned in a previous chapter; the other is Hod Hill (*Plate 12*). The most impressive remains of these sites are the massive multiple ramparts that enclose the plateau at the summit of each hill. Also visible within Hod Hill are the traces of a Roman fort that was inserted behind the inner rampart. The remaining features of the interior have been honed flat by centuries of agriculture, with the exception of one corner within the Hod Hill ramparts. Here, something of the earlier topography survives, protected from the ravages of the plough.

This area is crammed with ring-shaped earthworks, the remains of the round houses with which the hillfort was densely packed. While round houses had been a familiar feature of the landscape for several centuries, such a density of buildings in a single area was a new feature.

Few hillforts are as well preserved as this, and what projected above ground has generally disappeared. Even so, the subsoil features retain some measure of the intensity of activity within these sites. At Danebury, near Stockbridge in Hampshire, Barry Cunliffe has mounted a long-term project to expose the interior of a hillfort in its entirety, an area of just over 5ha (13 acres). After ten years of the project, less than a quarter had been exposed, yet this area alone was found to contain over 1000 disused storage pits. Vast numbers of postholes were also found, as well as interior roadways or tracks. In hillforts such as these, we are clearly seeing the beginnings of that most artificial of human environments, the urban landscape. It is to the environments created when human beings gather together in great numbers to which we turn in this chapter.

HUMAN COMMUNITIES: A QUESTION OF SCALE

Before focusing in on the development of sites such as Danebury, we must pause to consider what demands the basic requirements of life place on the way in which individuals cooperate, and the extent to which they gather together in groups of various sizes.

Many aspects of survival can be accomplished by individuals, or small

Figure 27 Map of locations
cited in Chapter 6.

Plate 12 Aerial view of Hod Hill, showing the earthen banks of the late prehistoric hillfort, traces of the round houses that survive in the south-eastern quadrant (towards the camera), and of the Roman fort that nestles in the north-western quadrant (away from the camera) (photo: RCHME).

family groups. Indeed healthy individuals, with access to sufficient land and exposure to an amenable climate, are well able at certain times to cope with the maintenance of a food supply ample for their own survival, and erect shelter in some form. The problems of food production, however, fluctuate through time.

In the short term there are seasonal fluctuations in the manpower required to maintain an agricultural plot. More people, for example, may be needed at harvest time when the crops must be gathered in fast before the rains. This has traditionally been a season in which the workforce is supplemented by drawing on the wider community.

In the longer term farmers must cope with the variation of human fitness within a single lifespan. During childhood, childbirth, sickness and old age, the dependency of individuals on each other may increase. Working from a massive survey of Russian peasants living in the late nineteenth and early twentieth centuries, Cheyenov demonstrated that even an extended family in relative economic isolation could experience considerable fluctuations in productivity and prosperity in relation to its changing internal age structure. A further long-term interdependency can arise from the need to spread the effects of crop failure and famine by communal storage of food.

The problems of self-sufficiency do not stop at shelter and food production. A group must also be able to reproduce successfully. Considering the time and energy invested in the acquisition of sexual partners in contemporary societies, including our own, it is surprising how often this crucial aspect of survival is overlooked in prehistoric societies.

The needs of successful reproduction place far greater demands on group size than the needs of basic production. Although human groups that tolerate a great deal of inbreeding are known, breeding populations would normally number several hundred at least, such that incest could be avoided. The maintenance of outbreeding in human groups frequently involves the ritualised gathering of substantial numbers of people, be it at a seasonal camp, a fair, or a discotheque.

A similar thing may be said of domestic animals. A family with one or two cattle, that are used for traction and the provision of dairy produce for the family, must make some provision for their eventual replacement. It would be both impossible and absurdly wasteful for each family to keep herds and flocks that are sufficiently large for populations to be maintained internally. They must therefore link into larger animal populations, and this either means the existence of some form of animal market, or a network of social interdependency between users of animals.

These points are concerned with biological needs alone. Past human communities would have had additional social needs, also involving the collaboration and gathering together of large groups, and such gathering would, of course, allow exchange of material items to take place. We must, therefore, think of the gathering together of such groups, not as an urban artefact, but as a regular feature of human behaviour.

We saw evidence of such gathering on a small scale by hunter-gatherers on the banks of the ancient lake of Pickering in Yorkshire. Seasonal gathering of hunter-gatherers was often synchronised with the similar behaviour of their prey. The American High Plains Indians, for example, while following the scattered buffalo for most of the year, collected together to camp around the full herd, and the overall gathering served both species.

Early farmers in England collected for feasts and to celebrate the dead in causewayed enclosures that served whole territories. In certain cases, such as at Hambledon Hill, Hembury, and Maiden Castle, these enclosures were overlain by the much later hillforts, perhaps hinting at their continued use as gathering points in the intervening millennia.

What is new about hillforts is the unprecedented density of archaeological material within them. The causewayed enclosures may in some cases have been occupied all year round by a small caretaker group, but the impression gained from the evidence from sites like Danebury is of large numbers of people remaining there for long periods, and perhaps permanently. It seems that by this period, human interaction had led to fixed permanent gatherings, just as in an earlier period, the relations of agricultural production had led to fixed, permanent land enclosure. To explore what was going on in more detail, we must turn to examine the results of the Danebury project.

DANEBURY: A HILLFORT IN HAMPSHIRE

The embanked hilltop enclosure at Danebury, near Stockbridge, sits perched on chalk downland between the River Test and the Wallop Brook. From the air we can see two ditched boundaries running from the enclosure, and an extensive patchwork of Celtic fields on the surrounding Downs. The structure of the fort's interior has been revealed by excavation.

The earliest phase of the hillfort reflects the gathering together not so much of people as of produce. The first features on this and other hillforts that were occupied before the fifth century BC are a series of square structures, 2–3m (7–10ft) across, defined by a group of postholes which are massive in relation to the ground area between them. They are believed to be the remains of raised storehouses. Perhaps these hillforts started out as central storage areas, taking in the grain from the extensive land enclosures with which they were intimately linked, and buffering members of the community against individual crop failure, and more general famine. We can follow the grain crops more closely, as their charred remains occur plentifully in every excavated feature on the site.

The gathering of crops

As we have seen in earlier chapters, the only plant remains that survive centuries of burial in a chalkland landscape are those that have been charred in a fire, such as charcoal and charred seeds. Such fragments may be difficult to see while the deposits are being dug, but when samples of these deposits are mixed in a large bin with water, the light charred material rises to the water's surface. From here it can be collected by decanting the surface water through a fine sieve, and studied under a microscope.

The composition of charred fragments at Danebury varies from place to place, but in every case they contain some pieces of cereal, usually together with seeds from the weeds that grew among the crop. The site is much richer in these fragments than the earlier sites discussed in the previous two chapters, and reflects a rather different picture of agricultural activity. By seeing exactly what was in each deposit, we can get some idea of what activities were taking place in and around the hillfort.

Charred remains may occur as mixtures of grains, chaff and weed seeds, found in roughly the same proportions as they would be found in

a growing field of cereals, thinly dispersed within an archaeological deposit. Such mixtures most likely correspond to the waste from a newly gathered harvest, swept up and thrown on the fire.

Then there are groups that are dominated by those same weed seeds, but in this case in association with much fewer cereals. Here, the weed seeds have clearly been cleaned from the grain by sieving, and the small seed impurities that fell through the sieve were again thrown on the fire. A third type of composition also relates to the processing of the crop. In this case, the fragments are dominated by a type of chaff, that would have been removed by pounding the ears with a large pestle and mortar.

Finally, deposits of cleaned grains are encountered, reflecting the waste from storage prior to milling and consumption. The excavations

Plate 13 Aerial view of the hillfort at Danebury, with the clean chalk surface of the excavations in view (photo: RCHME).

also produced nearly 600 pieces of 'querns', the stones used to mill the grains.

As has already been said, charred remains of these kinds are found everywhere and in every deposit of refuse on the site. We get the impression of a bustle of activity, with cartloads of freshly harvested grain moving along the central track within the fort, and people everywhere pounding, sieving, and preparing the grain for storage. Where all this grain comes from we can explore by taking a closer look at the weeds found with them.

Figure 28 The processing of prehistoric crops. A typical sequence of stages in the handling of a cereal such as spelt wheat in the first millennium BC. Threshing separates the seed heads from the straw. Winnowing allows the wind to carry away the lighter chaff and feathery weed seeds. Sieving separates off the very small and very large weed seeds and chaff fragments. Pounding liberates the grain from its very closely bound chaff envelope. Each stage leaves a characteristic set of debris in the archaeological record.

The seeds of over 40 different types of weed were found together with the charred cereal grains. Many we can imagine in among today's crops on the downs: carpets of red poppies up above a tangle of purple fumitory, and with docks, fathen and a multitude of wild grasses poking above the heads of cereals. Corn marigold and sheep's sorrel normally flourish on soils that are more acid than those found around Danebury today. The few seeds of these plants are likely to have come from where there was a capping of acid clay over the chalk. There are also, among the charred debris, seeds of plants of damp ground, sedges, mint and others. These must have come some distance to the fort, from locations along the neighbouring river valleys, a few kilometres from the site.

So not only do these charred fragments give us some clue as to the range of activities going on within the site, they also provide an idea of the catchment from which the crops were brought.

Just as charred seeds are everywhere, so are animal bones prolific on the site. The first ten years of excavation produced nearly 140,000 fragments. This in itself shows that animals were brought to the site to be consumed, and it also provides a picture of the range of animals brought in. Sheep are by far the commonest, and we may imagine stretches of chalk grassland around Danebury with flocks grazing upon them. Cattle are the next most frequent species, followed by pigs. Annie Grant, who studied the bones in relation to the surrounding landscape, suggested that the cattle would have seasonally grazed in the river meadows, and the pigs would have been put to mast in woodland. Her work involved not just the identification of species, but also the age of the animals at death. This is done by looking at various parts of the bones and teeth that markedly change their form during one life span.

One interesting point about the ageing of these animal bones was that the bones of sheep, cattle and pig each included examples that had died at birth. We would not expect to find such bones far from where birth took place, and this suggests that with all three species, breeding took place within the hillfort. This reminds us that one of the purposes of gathering together in numbers is to maintain successful reproduction among human and domestic animal populations.

The same does not appear to be true of the horse bones, which notably lack a component of animals that died young. The rarity of foals on this and other sites has prompted the suggestion that horses were not bred, but instead periodically rounded up from wild populations that roamed the Wessex chalklands of prehistory.

The gathering of people

As the millennium progressed, so the evidence of human activity within the fort increased. Large pits for underground storage began to proliferate soon after the hillfort was established, and round houses were built in the lee of the rampart. Through time, houses spread to fill the northern sector of the interior. Side roads appeared in the southern part, lined with raised storehouses to receive goods from the traffic on those roads.

Figure 29 The pattern of agricultural and other resources entering the hillfort at Danebury (information from B. Cunliffe 1984 *Danebury: an Iron Age Hillfort in Hampshire*).

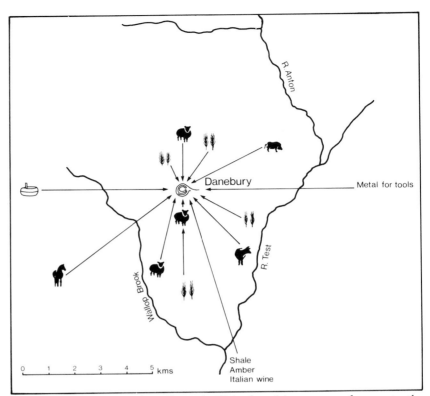

The ramparts were heavily embellished at this stage, and entry to the site was through the maze of substantial earthworks visible to the east of the site today. Passing through this entrance, sheep and cattle might be seen coralled between the ramparts on either side. Inside the entrance within the busy cluster of thatched wattle and daub houses, back yards, and storehouses raised on timber stilts, the flint cobbling of the main route through the site would stretch out ahead leading to a group of shrines at the centre of the fort. Several hundred people would be living and working in the interior, and crops and livestock would be brought in from thousands of hectares around the site. Other goods would be brought from even further afield.

Goods from afar

The hillfort's inhabitants made extensive use of stone, as whetstones to sharpen their sickles, querns to grind their corn, and weights to regulate exchange and tribute. Thousands of fragments of such implements were recovered from the excavations. It was clear from an analysis of these fragments that they were brought in from over 30km (18½ miles), and in some cases up to 80km (50 miles) to the west of the site. Salt was brought in in clay containers from the Dorset and Hampshire coasts, and fragments of the disused salt containers are common among the rubbish within the fort. Metals, in particular iron, were used for sickles, ploughshares, woodworking equipment, horse fittings, ornament and for a variety of other purposes. Trace elements within the iron indicate that much of the iron may have derived from the Wealden clay beds 90km (56 miles) to the east, and similar work on the bronze suggests an equally distant origin.

Luxury and ornamental items of shale, coral and amber also reflect movement over long distances, though of fairly small quantities. Another luxury that was reaching the site towards the end of its life was Italian wine.

We can follow both the presence of continental wine amphorae, and the shrinkage of the hillfort, to explore the new kinds of gathering place that replaced many of the hillforts towards the end of the first millennium BC.

The original location of this and other hillforts had been well suited to the movement of people and products within the immediate agricultural landscape. They were, however, generally located at some distance from the waterways that were becoming increasingly important as the volume of long-distance trade expanded in the later stages of the first millennium BC.

Along these waterways a new series of embanked enclosures was growing up, often of a greater size than the hillforts of which many, like Danebury, were going into decline. These lowlying sites, often described as 'oppida', formed the focus of a landscape in which movement of goods and people was to occur on an unprecendented scale.

None of these oppida has received the kind of extensive excavation to which Danebury has been subjected, and so we must guess at their internal layout from fieldwalking and aerial photography. Cropmarks within the Dyke Hills site at Dorchester-on-Thames in Oxfordshire, for example, show an interior broken up by ditched enclosures, and scattered with round house gullies, pits and ditches. The larger oppida may also enclose extensive open areas. An important point to note is that these large low-lying defended sites appear along rivers in the south and east of England, and that at the same time, those areas also produce England's first coins and wine amphorae, hallmarks of a network of links that stretched across the continent from Rome.

The connection with Rome led to the appearance of written accounts of contact with Britain, such as those of Julius Caesar's exploratory visits to the islands. We can read Caesar and Suetonius who actually used the word 'oppidum' for settlements in Britain. We learn of tribes and a series of tribal chieftains.

The wine that arrived in this country from the Mediterranean not surprisingly ended up with these chieftains. Wine amphorae have been found in the graves of a number of such chieftains around Essex and Hertfordshire, along with Italian bronze vessels, silver cups and brooches. For the goods that were exchanged to acquire such luxuries, we are fortunate enough to have a contemporary record compiled by a Greek geographer named Strabo, listing Britain's exports. They were: corn, cattle, gold, silver, hides, slaves, and hunting dogs. So it seems that these oppida, like the earlier hillforts, were gathering points for the agricultural produce of the surrounding landscape, part of which went, together with rare metals and some of the less fortunate inhabitants of that landscape, to pay for the luxuries enjoyed by the powerful.

Powerful these chieftains may have been, but their power was to be dwarfed by another force that emanated from the Mediterranean together with the stocks of wine and fancy metalwork. During the course of the first century AD, most of what was to become England was incorporated within the massive empire of Rome.

GATHERING TOGETHER WITHIN THE ROMAN EMPIRE

Urban settlement was a crucial element of the workings of the Roman Empire for a number of reasons. One of the ways the Empire expanded was through the settlement of army veterans in 'coloniae' in newly absorbed territory. The settlers, each with a small plot of land within the territory of the colonia, established a firm Roman presence in alien territory. In the first few years after the Conquest, such a colonia was established at Colchester, and by the end of the century, a further two had been established at Gloucester and Lincoln.

Towns also functioned as the administrative centres within the Empire. So, just as in nineteenth-century Africa a fluid network of tribal alliances was tied to fixed areas of land, for the expediency of Europian colonial administrations, so were the tribes encountered in Britain organised in territories around 'civitas capitals' by the Roman administration.

In addition to these active steps towards urbanisation, the nature of Roman expansion itself led to the creation of gatherings of population within the landscape. The Roman army was huge in relation to the size of the populations with which it was contending. Up to 70,000 troops were used in Britain, whose total population was but a few million. The troops were housed in a string of forts within the expanding frontier zone.

From aerial photography, we see, adjacent to many of these forts, the appearance of a cluster of buildings outside the military installations themselves. We know little of how these 'vici' developed, but their economic life must surely have been closely linked to the needs and desires of those within the forts. We can envisage the local population around these forts collecting within the vici to provide a range of services to the soldiers.

The Antonine Itinery, an official route-list compiled in the early third century, lists over 70 urban centres stretching from Canterbury to Carlisle. Many of these sites are towns today, and the famous network of roads that linked them in the Roman period, in many cases still links them today. These records bear witness to the impact of the Empire on the English landscape. Yet the closer we look at the evidence for these components of the urban landscape in the Roman period, the more it seems these developments mark changes in scale rather than direction.

Urban settlement before and after the Conquest

Although many of the Roman sites were imposed on the landscape, their location was governed by pre-existing sites. The colonia at Colchester, for example, was located on the site of a pre-existing legionary fortress, itself positioned to police the oppidum of Camelodunum. In this way, Colchester remained a focus of population through the Conquest. The other coloniae, Gloucester, Lincoln and York, were also placed over or nearby sites previously occupied by legionary forts, themselves located in relation to the existing population.

The administrative centres, or civitas capitals, similarly tended to reflect the pre-existing foci within the landscape. The development was often similar to Colchester: a military site was established near to a centre of population, and the military site itself was developed to form the administrative centre. Such could have been the case with, for example, Cirencester, 5 km (3 miles) from the oppidum at Bagendon, and Dorchester, 4 km ($2\frac{1}{2}$ miles) from the hillfort at Maiden Castle.

Where the population was more easily subsumed into Roman control, the administrative capital could actually be created within a pre-existing settlement, as at the site of Silchester. In this way a great deal of the map of Roman towns in Britain reflected the underlying skeleton of foci of population within the pre-existing landscape. We might muse that some of the roads linking those centres followed the line of previously established routes.

Changes of scale

However much the urban landscape of the Roman period followed a pre-existing pattern, there can be no doubt of the increase in scale with which this affected the landscape. The number of urban centres increased, as did the numbers of people moving in and out of them, and the range from which people and produce came expanded.

Before the Conquest we have evidence, in the form of amphorae, of agricultural products such as wine arriving from the Mediterranean. Soon after the Conquest, the list of exotic products found in English towns lengthens. The earliest colonia at Colchester was soon to start receiving figs, raisins, olives, mulberries, walnuts and dates. By the second century, London was receiving many of these, and in addition peaches, pine nuts, and cucumber. Figs and raisins seem to appear at every Roman town from London to Carlisle that has the waterlogged deposits to preserve them. Together with these more conspicuous imports, we must imagine a whole range of plants and animals being brought into towns with agricultural produce, fuel, building materials, and inadvertently on wheels, boots, hoofs, in the back of carts, and along rivers and canals.

Indeed the list of species that accumulates in some form or other within an urban landscape can get very long. To take but one example, a Roman well, excavated within the colonia of York at Skeldergate, contained within its waterlogged fill fragments of over 140 species of plants, over 300 species of beetles and bugs, nearly 50 species of mites, and a miscellaneous selection of vertebrates, molluscs, spiders and other animals.

This underlines a point made by the ecologist Eugene Odum; we may think of urban landscapes as being, in ecological terms, rather sterile in comparison with the countryside, but in fact they can be extremely rich environments, on account of the continual import of material from a variety of habitats. A well-worn street, lined by buildings, may seem barren of plants and animals. Yet enough seeds will be lying dormant to bring a vacant lot to life, and attract a wide range of small animals from around. A crevice within a wall, or a roof of turf or thatch will provide a niche for countless plants and animals.

Species may also be encouraged consciously, for aesthetic reasons. It is in the Roman period that we have the first clear evidence of decorative plants, and the construction of elaborate gardens. We also know from microscopic analyses of the sediments that built up within many Roman towns, that the soil and compost were actively brought into these towns to create garden plots and allotments. These are the sediments that form the 'dark earths' found in the later Roman levels of several towns.

Ecological enrichment of a landscape is, however, not always aesthetically pleasing. If we return to the concept of the ecological pyramid, introduced in the second chapter, we can construct such a pyramid for an early urban ecosystem. Dominating the bottom level is imported foodstuffs and materials for building, bedding and fuel. At the second level are the humans and domestic animals kept within the site. But the massive import of all kinds of biological materials encouraged that ecological pyramid to expand both in breadth and in height. Many of the loose ends of this pyramid were no doubt cleaned up by dogs and pigs, but these animals were not alone. At the apex of the pyramid were some fairly unsavoury creatures.

The pyramid's unsavoury apex: weevils, rats and worms
The York Archaeological Trust has conducted a number of excavations within the City of York, which have provided us with some of our clearest insights into early urban environments. One such excavation in Coney Street was conducted on an early Roman warehouse that lay between the legionary fort at York and the River Ouse.

In some places, traces of the timber foundations remained; elsewhere their position was marked by the slots they once occupied. The ground around these slots was sufficiently waterlogged to preserve the debris from the warehouse that slurried into them. This debris was rich in the fragmented remains of Roman beetles, and over 99 per cent of these beetles were grain pests. Harry Kenward's detailed analysis of these beetles provides us with a valuable insight into the problems that faced those attempting to collect together and handle unprecedented quantities of grain.

The golden opportunity provided by their attempt did not go unnoticed by the remainder of the animal kingdom. Among the chief opportunists were the saw-toothed grain beetle, the rust-red grain

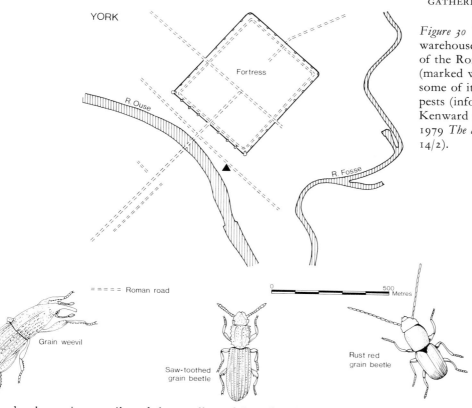

Figure 30 The Coney Street warehouse at York. Position of the Roman grain store (marked with a triangle) and some of its most virulent pests (information from H. Kenward and D. Williams 1979 *The archaeology of York* 14/2).

beetle, the grain weevil, and the small-eyed flour beetle, species that had most probably followed the Roman army across Europe in their food provisions. It seems there were enough of these and other grain-eating insects to reduce whole warehouses full of grain to 'tattered husks and powdery frass'.

Elsewhere in York, we can find other species at the unsavoury apex of the ecological pyramid. Among the many species recorded from the Skeldergate well cited above were a few bones of the black rat, a creature subsequently associated with bubonic plague.

Diseases and parasites are also encouraged by the gathering together of humans, and indeed any species, in concentrated populations. Bacteria and viruses generally elude the archaeological record, but with larger parasites we can begin to detect their presence in the past.

Just within the walls of the legionary fortress at York runs a stone-lined sewer, draining between modern Swinegate and Church Street. Like so many other sites at York, the excavations yielded waterlogged biological remains in abundance. Alongside a wide range of plant remains, insects, snails and small vertebrates were the eggs of two rather unpleasant types of worm. These are *Trichuris*, the threadlike 'whip-worm' and the larger *Ascaris* or 'maw-worm' which can reach over 30cm (12in) in length. Both inhabit the human gut, sometimes in horrifying numbers, and can lead to a range of gut problems, nausea and anaemia.

While the various sites excavated within Roman York have provided a hint of the ecological problems of gathering together, to witness the full force of ecological opportunism within the urban landscape, we must follow these towns into the post-Roman period.

Anglo-Saxon and Viking towns

As the Roman presence in Britain faded, so did much of its urban infrastructure. Those towns and settlements most closely bound up with the Roman administration declined markedly, and several civitas capitals have never regained the status of major towns. Many of the smaller Roman towns owed their existence to more local economic forces, and were therefore less vulnerable to the collapse of the Empire.

In general terms, the urban landscape shrank considerably after the breakdown of Roman rule in the fifth century. Many towns had already adopted a more rural aspect, by creating allotments and coralling animals within the town, and the deposition of dark earth, which results from these activities, continued to spread over the abandoned building plots. Between the fifth and eighth centuries, we have little more than these dark earth deposits as records of what remained of the urban landscape.

When towns grew again later in the first millennium, many of them grew within the old Roman towns. If this was not to do with surviving nuclei of settlement, then the choices of location may instead have been dictated by ease of defence, and the efficient network of communication that survived around the old centres. The true nature of English towns during the Dark Age is a topic to which recent and current archaeology is fast adding new evidence, and the picture may change dramatically. Environmental archaeology at towns such as York is also progressing fast, and allowing us to compare and contrast towns of the later first millennium with their Roman predecessors.

Anglo-Scandinavian York

In comparison with the Roman fortress and colonia, the town that had grown by the ninth century was dirty. In contrast to the relatively clean, mineral sediments of Roman York, the Anglo-Scandinavian levels are generally rich in rotting organic matter, and the plant and animal life preserved within it elaborate the picture. Among the plants that colonised roadsides and vacant lots were such species as elder and fathen, plants that thrive in the conditions of high nitrogen and phosphorus that accompany rotting compost, excrement and other organic waste.

Flies swarmed around, and earwigs and beetles crawled in and out of murky corners; their remains and those of hundreds of other insects are preserved in the waterlogged deposits in the town. Insects are perhaps the best indicators of filth, stagnation and squalor: they are very discerning about particular subdivisions of these categories. For example, different groups of insects will be attracted to dry, fibrous compost and moist, putrid compost. Such detail can add a great deal of colour to our reconstructions of early urban landscapes!

Various categories of decaying material were clearly to be found, and this was reflected in the state of health in the town. The townspeople suffered from fleas, and, like their Roman predecessors, from intestinal worms. Andrew Jones' study of these parasites has produced striking results; not only were they present, the town was riddled with them. Even the floors inside houses contained staggering numbers of worm eggs, ready to hatch inside some unfortunate host. The highest concentrations came, not surprisingly, from cess pits, and in one case from an intact human stool. This exciting find was estimated to contain over a million roundworm eggs. The person who passed it must have carried in their gut at least a small number of maw-worms, and several hundred whip-worms. Today this would be classed as a heavy infection.

It seems likely that the townspeople of ninth- and tenth-century York would have regarded a moderate infestation of intestinal worms as quite normal, and the same was presumably true of a much broader range of infections that have left no archaeological trace.

So in the two millennia that separate the earliest hillforts from England's medieval towns, we can follow the development of a very specialised environment that began with the gathering together of agricultural produce for storage, and became a dense gathering of people and of goods from afar, and then a gathering of the scavengers and parasites that thrive on such a rich conflux of life. The landscape had become divided into town and country, and the inhabitants of one saw themselves as distinct from the other, viewing their counterparts with envy, uncertainty, humour or scorn.

Yet the two were tightly interlinked. We have seen how the very vitality of the town depended on the enormous influx of goods from the countryside, and at first this dependency may seem to be one way only. The rural population were, after all, capable of producing their own food and shelter. A closer inspection, however, reveals their many strands of dependency on the urban centres with which they co-existed, and, in some senses, the rural landscape that surrounded these developing towns was no less an artefact than the urban environment itself. To this topic we shall turn in the next chapter.

7

Smallholdings and survival

Through the millennia that followed the last glacial retreat, we have seen the human population become gradually less elusive. One by one, a range of human activities has been fixed within the landscape so as to leave a permanent imprint on the archaeological record. In turn, the monuments to their dead and the boundaries around their land assumed a permanence in space that would persist for centuries. The activities that remained notoriously elusive until quite late in prehistory were sheltering and sleeping; in other words, we have had great difficulty in locating the rural dwelling places of prehistory.

Not until the later part of the second millennium BC is the number of known dwellings in any way consistent with the intensity of human activity that is evident in the contemporary landscape. It may be that we have been looking in the wrong places, and that early settlements lie buried beneath valley sediments, for example. It may be that shelter and sleeping were catered for in structures that leave no archaeological trace. The answer may lie in a combination of such factors. What little evidence we have we can nevertheless draw together and contrast it with the abundant evidence of rural dwellings that appears in the course of the first millennium BC.

EARLY FARMING SETTLEMENT

England before the third millennium BC offers little more in the way of settlement evidence than scatters of postholes, together with pits full of domestic rubbish, and a scatter of flint across the soil surface. Traces of a few small rectangular structures survive, perhaps the bases of log cabins of the early farmers. By the end of the third millennium, however, we begin to find evidence of the round houses which were to form a major part of vernacular architecture for the next 2000 years.

Some idea of the appearance of England's prehistoric round houses can be gained by visiting the Butser Ancient Farmstead at the Queen Elizabeth Park just south of Petersfield in Hampshire. Here, Peter Reynolds has reconstructed a number of such buildings within a contemporary agrarian setting. Lofty conical thatched roofs rise to a steep point above circular walls of wattle and daub. They may vary between modest huts a few metres across, to impressive and spacious buildings, 20m (66ft) and more in diameter. In different parts of the

Figure 31 Map of locations cited in Chapter 7.

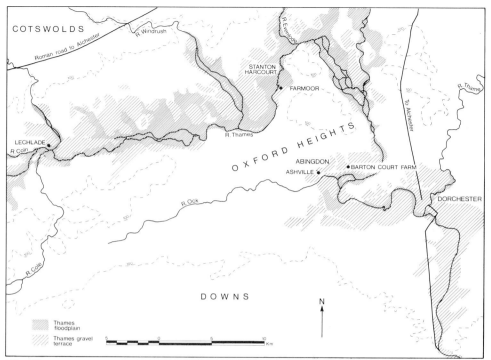

Figure 32 The Upper
Thames Valley: map of sites
mentioned in the text.

country, walls would have been of stone rather than wattle and daub,
and turf and heather might have been used in place of straw or reed
thatch, but the common theme across the human landscape would have
been these lofty conical roofs.

Through the course of the second millennium a series of rural
dwelling places leave their mark, and as the extensive systems of land
enclosure described in Chapter 5 appear in the landscape, so these
dwellings are found interlocking with them. The clearest examples are
found within the reeve systems on Dartmoor, such as the
'neighbourhood group' of houses strung out beneath the terminal reeve
on Holne Moor. The chalk downlands of the south and east also have
settlements interlocking with field systems. The layout of sites such as
Itford Hill, New Barn Down and Black Patch in Sussex, and South
Lodge and Martin Down on Cranbourne Chase, reflects their
incorporation into the broader systems of land division that surround
them. It seems likely that, both on the chalk downs and on Dartmoor,
the same forces that led to the coordinated division of land also provided
a means of linkage between these scattered dwellings, so vital in the
sustenance of human and animal reproduction, survival over lean years,
and the exchange of goods and social intercourse.

In addition to such 'nested' settlements, we begin to see sites laid out
in a manner that suggests that they were conceived on an individual
basis. Fields are added piecemeal on the borders of parallel systems, and
groups of round houses appear within enclosures that bear no obvious
relation to any grander plan. In some cases, this need not imply a

departure from the overall coordinated scheme; there is no reason to suppose, for example, that the detached hut groups beyond the parallel reeve systems on Dartmoor existed in isolation from them. Yet as we move from the second millennium to the first millennium BC there does seem to be a marked trend away from nested and towards detached settlement layout. Within this latter group, there are a very large number of known sites, and a great deal of variety in form both within and between regions.

There are individual round houses with one or two out-buildings and storage pits, all encircled by a ditch, fence or wall enclosing a hectare or so. There are also small unenclosed groups of closely packed round houses, together with clusters of storage pits. We are discovering new forms of late prehistoric settlement all the time, and the picture that is emerging of rural England in the first millennium BC is of a rich and varied landscape of homesteads and hamlets, filling the river valleys and spreading out across the hillslopes.

In order to piece together the workings of such landscapes, we can begin with a region whose rural prehistoric settlement is now relatively well known, as a result of the work of the Oxford Archaeological Unit.

RURAL SETTLEMENT IN THE UPPER THAMES VALLEY

The River Thames arises from a series of streams draining south from the Cotswold slopes in Gloucestershire. In the early first millennium BC, these streams would have run through a patchwork of woodland and scrubby grassland into a relatively open landscape; it seems from the pollen evidence that we have, that the floodplain of the upper Thames had lost its wildwood at a fairly early stage. In many places the stretches of grassland that line the Thames today were already established.

If we walk along the river's upper reaches today, we can see, in addition to its modern tributaries, a whole series of dry channels meandering across the valley bottom. Prior to when the river's drainage was controlled by canalisation and locks, these same channels would have born a multitude of streams. The waterlogged silts that have since filled them up are a major source of the biological evidence that allows us to reconstruct the settled, heavily grazed pastoral landscape of the first millennium BC.

With aerial photography and fieldwalking, we can supplement this picture of an open, grassy landscape with the small settlements that arose during the first millennium BC. Just west of Lechlade, a whole stretch of this landscape has been excavated. Nestling between the meandering streams on each dry patch of ground was a small group of round houses and their associated paddocks.

Following the river downstream, we would pass the conical roofs and fenced paddocks of whole series of scattered settlements, and in the lush grassland around, their grazing livestock would be seen. The river valley would gradually widen out, its sides forming a sequence of flat, stepped terraces. Some of the houses on these terraces would be fixed and permanent, set within hedged enclosures; others would be very temporary indeed.

A group of the more temporary dwellings was discovered and excavated about 30km (18½ miles) downstream from Lechlade, just below Wytham Hill at Farmoor. Here, on the broad floodplain of the river, were found the ditches and postholes of a series of round houses with their associated paddocks. Because the sites were low-lying, a rich variety of biological remains was preserved in the waterlogged fills of the features.

Among the remains were the shells of minute freshwater snails. They were too small to have been brought there intentionally, and must have travelled there in floodwaters. The fine sediments that cover the site also bear witness to these floods. While studying the ditch deposits, Mark Robinson noticed that the weed seeds present were from annual plants; the perennial weeds that flourish on other sites were not to be found. All this evidence points to fairly ephemeral settlement, between periods of flooding, and not disturbing the ground for long enough for perennial weeds to take hold. In other words, at Farmoor we seem to have the traces of the shortlived summer shelters of those who came to graze their animals on the lush summer growth, and then return in winter to higher ground.

The seeds preserved in the waterlogged deposits give some idea of the plants that grew within the seasonally inundated grassy sward to which these animals were brought. The tall stems of meadowsweet and dock would have coloured the green pasture with patches of white and ruddy brown. In among clusters of rush stems closer to the ground, the pink, purple and yellow flowers of ragged robin, self-heal, buttercup and silverweed could have been seen. The occasional presence of kingcups and greater burnet might be linked with the cutting of hay, but we have no firm evidence of hay-cutting on these banks until the Roman period, when some fragments of cut hay and a discarded scythe appear in Farmoor's archaeological record. The same deposits that preserved seeds of these and many other plants also preserved numerous fragments of dung-beetles, reflecting another component that would have added both colour and odour to the Farmoor landscape.

Not surprisingly, the archaeological remains for both the seasonal shelters at Farmoor and the more permanent dwellings close to the river, such as at Lechlade, are associated with numerous animal bones. In each case the predominance of cattle bones suggests that these were the major form of livestock grazing the open stretches of riverside pasture.

Each of these low-lying sites also contains small quantities of cereal chaff and weeds along with fragments of quernstone at Lechlade. So although set within a pastoral landscape, the inhabitants were eating at least small quantities of grain, and we may ask from where it came.

The answer may be found, not on the floodplain itself, but on the better drained gravel terraces above the floodplain. On one such terrace, about 20km (12½ miles) further downstream, another form of first-millennium settlement has been excavated, lying just off the Thames on a side tributary, the river Ock. Like the other sites, it consisted of traces of a group of round houses, this time associated with a cluster of storage pits rather than paddocks.

On this drier site, known as the Ashville Site, waterlogged deposits are scarce, and the main biological materials are animal bones and charred plant remains, and each of these shows marked differences from the floodplain sites.

First, the bones are dominated by sheep rather than cattle, and indeed just north of the site the ground rises onto a limestone slope well-suited to sheep grazing. Secondly, the charred plant remains are not composed, like the floodplain sites, of small quantities of cereal chaff and weeds; they are instead made up of vast quantities of chaff, weeds and grain. In each deposit excavated, thousands of such fragments could be found. It seems that when the site was occupied, every scatter of refuse swept up and thrown on the fire contained cereal debris.

We can imagine the settlement in late summer, littered with the spill of the harvest, and even some of the grains themselves getting into the settlement fires. It seems we are dealing with a settlement able to produce a surplus of cereals, and with provision for underground storage of the crop in the form of a cluster of pits.

Apart from these differences in quantity, the charred remains on the higher terrace sites and the floodplain site are very similar, with the same crops and the same weeds occurring in both areas. We can infer that crops were being taken down from the higher sites, where they grew well, to the pastoral settlements on the floodplain. Presumably the grazing animals were moving in the opposite direction.

Several sites of the first millennium BC have now been examined in the Upper Thames Valley, both on its floodplain and on the various gravel terraces that rise alongside it. They vary a great deal in terms of their layout and internal organisation, and in terms of how they exploited the landscape. Yet, while individual in form, the links of interdependency are clear. A close look at the three sites described above showed that they were by no means isolated homesteads. People, livestock and crops were all moving from one part of the landscape to another. Other things were also moving.

One example is salt. The upper Thames is about as far from natural sources of salt as it is possible to be in England. Yet among the fragments from the Lechlade site are the pottery containers from which salt was brought from as far afield as Cheshire.

In addition to perishable goods and people, durable materials were moved around. At each site the farming communities used implements of metal and stone. This involved bringing in materials from afar; some of the quernstones used at Lechlade were of Derbyshire rock. It also involved access to craft-working skills. At the Ashville site, not only do we find rivets, knives, and a small sickle made of iron, but we also find fragments of crucible and slag, and two working hollows where the smiths prepared and heated their materials.

It is hard to tell whether these were the debris of a travelling blacksmith, or whether the farmers took care of small-scale metal-working themselves, but either way, the social network existed within the rural community, along which either specialist knowledge or the specialists themselves could travel. As a result, we see in the first millennium BC a gradual expansion in the utilitarian application of metal technology.

So although we have characterised these first millennium settlements as being detached from any large-scale system of land division, the excavated evidence reveals the multitude of strands that linked them, involving people, specialist knowledge, materials, livestock and agricultural produce. Many of these links were between sites within the valley.

Indeed, although we have contrasted detached settlements such as these with the earlier nested settlements within the Dartmoor reeves, they share with these earlier settlements the tendency to cluster into neighbourhood groups. Around Lechlade, Stanton Harcourt and Abingdon respectively, we can find such groups, each of about 30 sites.

Other links would have involved networks spreading across a much larger area, and for these we might look above the valley to the hills on either side, and the hillforts strung out along them. The chalk downlands to the south, and the Cotswolds and Oxford Heights to the north and west are each crowned by a series of such forts, which we can imagine were gathering places for regional exchanges of goods and social intercourse.

It may then be that the valley farmers turned in two directions for their community needs. They turned to one another for agricultural goods and access to grazing land, and to the wider network linking larger sites for salt, stone, iron, and the maintenance of human and animal reproduction.

SETTLEMENT ON THE HILLSLOPES

If we move from the valley to the areas of higher land to the north and south of the Upper Thames Valley, we see around the hillforts a different pattern of settlement. Again the small settlements have 'detached' plans, but they are more widely separated than in the valley and the huts and out-buildings are placed within a small enclosure.

Many of these enclosed farmsteads have been excavated, especially those that lie to the south, across the Wessex chalklands. We can take the example of a site on Winnall Down, just outside Winchester, where Peter Fasham's excavations have provided a detailed picture of the organisation of a site which in the middle of the first millennium BC was an enclosed farmstead.

An enclosed farmstead at Winnall Down
During this stage of the site's life, a modest ditch and bank enclosed around 0.5 ha ($1\frac{1}{4}$ acres) of chalk downland overlooking the river Itchen. On entering the enclosure through its western gateway, we would have

been guided by fences past the different areas within the enclosure, in which different activities were taking place.

Across to our right, farmers would be loading their harvest of six-row barley, spelt wheat and pulses into deep storage pits. Once filled, each pit would be sealed with clay, and could be left like that all winter. As soon as the pit seal was broken, the grain would be transferred to stilted granaries located near to the pits, and the week's flour ground by laboriously working to and fro on saddle querns.

Ahead of us, beyond the grain-processing compound, a craft-working area would be found. Bone and antler would be worked into combs, points, gouges and needles. A smith might be seen forging metal tools.

The main living quarters would be to our left. Outside the round houses, woollen cloth would have been woven on sturdy upright looms. We can still find their massive postholes and disused loomweights cast into a nearby rubbish pit. Another pit in this area contains the bones from three entire cows and two horses, bearing cut-marks showing where the limbs were disarticulated and the meat stripped off.

These farms were clearly providing for many of their own internal needs, but give the impression of grain production, weaving and meat culling on a scale that implies some exchange of goods. Their querns were brought in from a distance and use was made of metal objects such as iron nails.

Just as their contemporaries in the Thames Valley were involved in a network of interdependencies, so were the farmers of Winnall Down; but in this case the settlements were not clustered into neighbourhood groups, and the focal position of the more densely scattered hillforts may well have been more important.

Questions of scale

Each of the farming settlements described above may well have been occupied by no more than one extended family group. It might have been tempting to regard them as independent self-sufficient units, but, as was emphasised in the last chapter, such small groups would not have been able to operate in a truly self-sufficient manner; they must have been linked into some larger network, if for the needs of human and animal reproduction alone. As we have seen in this chapter, their involvement in wider networks entailed much more than just these basic elements. We have also speculated on how those wider networks might have worked. The detached settlements coexisted with the large hilltop enclosures where several families and their animals could gather together.

We might speculate that it was the immense flexibility of these large gatherings in terms of communal interaction that removed restrictions on the nature of rural settlement. Individual families would have been able to exist within discrete, dispersed homesteads, in the knowledge that there was somewhere to acquire new livestock, dispose of surplus, and to find prospective sexual partners. Without such centres of gathering and exchange, dispersed settlement could only exist within a clearly structured social landscape, such as we have seen existed in previous millennia.

A parallel can be drawn with what are today described as 'peasant communities'. These are rural communities that are divided up into families, who each produce the majority of the goods they individually consume. Peasant cultures have been described as 'half-cultures', as they almost invariably coexist with urban societies and markets. Even if used for no more than a fraction of their material needs, those markets provide a vital contact with a wider community. Without occasional contact of this sort, life in isolated small family groups could not be sustained.

The rural families of southern England in the first millennium may have conducted their affairs in a similar way to modern peasants. Most production and consumption was contained within the family household, but gathering places remained vital for reproduction and exchange. Just as urban centres are dependent on their rural hinterland, so might the detached rural settlements of the first millennium BC have been dependent on their hillforts.

An immediate problem with this model is that the kind of detached rural settlements we have been describing spread far further across England in the first millennium BC than did the contemporary hillforts.

BEYOND THE HILLFORT ZONE

A wide range of sites in the English landscape are described as hillforts, and many may be no more than enclosed farmsteads on hilltops. If we consider just the large, busy centres like Danebury, then they are heavily concentrated in the south and the west of the country. The River Test with its tributaries, for example, flows past six large hillforts besides Danebury in the space of 50km (30 miles). Such densities fall off rapidly to the north of the Chilterns and also to the east of the Welsh Marches.

Were we to travel up the Nene in the East Midlands, a river two to three times as long as the Test, we would reach almost to its source before encountering the hillforts at Hunsbury and Borough Hill. Yet along the way we would have passed around 70 known settlements of the first millennium BC. Further to the north, we would have to follow the tributaries of the River Humber right up to their Pennine sources, before reaching such lofty hillfort sites as Mam Tor, Almondbury and Ingleborough, and again we would have passed many known settlements on the way.

It may be that the seasonal journeys were made to these remote hillforts from considerable distances, and such journeys served many of the needs of community interaction. However, those areas where hillforts are sparse are clearly not remote backwaters. In the east of England, for example, there is considerable evidence during the first millennium of exchange networks linking the region with continental

Europe. It appears that recourse to a distant hillfort was by no means a prerequisite to social interaction.

David Knight's survey of settlements along the Nene and Great Ouse basins revealed a quite distinct clustering of sites into ten discrete zones. While this effect could be caused by uneven sampling, we may once again have a collection of neighbourhood groups, as in the Thames Valley, only this time playing a more dominant role in group interaction and exchange.

Another possible focus for rural communities in the East Midlands was what might have been an early form of village. This category of site is made up once again of round houses, but occurring in larger numbers than in the contemporary farmsteads. At Little Waltham in Essex, for example, a partial excavation revealed the ditches of 18 such buildings. At Fengate in the Nene Valley a cluster of features corresponds to about 55 buildings. One problem of interpreting these sites is that the impression of a cluster of buildings can be spuriously created by a single building rebuilt a few times on a slightly different plan – something that can be shown to have happened on a number of occasions. In other words, these 'villages' might in reality be shifting homesteads, and this would leave the problem of how rural settlements interacted in the east of the country, prior to the emergence of oppida, wide open.

The far north

In his commentary on the Gallic Wars, Caesar drew a distinction between a maritime part and an inland part of the British landscape. The maritime part corresponded to the area that had previously been colonised by Belgic tribes, and he records how 'after the invasion they abode there and began to till the fields'. In contrast to this, he says of the 'inlanders' who were presumably to be found further from the south-eastern shore, that 'most do not sow corn, but live on milk and flesh and clothe themselves in skins'.

Until quite recently, these comments were held to reflect a landscape in which arable agriculture was restricted to the south-east; the enclosed homesteads found in the north of the country were assumed to house the herders of cattle.

Indeed those that have been excavated have produced quantities of cattle bone, along with smaller amounts of sheep, pig and horse. But environmental archaeology has greatly expanded this picture, as can be seen in the region around the mouth of the River Tees.

This area has produced a number of pollen-bearing deposits, sufficient to show that even by the second millennium BC, extensive clearances had developed, in part for arable cultivation. There is also much evidence for woodland regeneration, and the general picture is of a shifting mosaic of woodland, pasture and arable land continuing through the first millennium BC.

During this period several farming settlements can be found in the archaeological record, and one that has been recently excavated lies between 5 to 10km (3 to 6 miles) north of the river at Thorpe Thewles.

Plate 14 The late prehistoric farmstead at Thorpe Thewles (from a painting by A. Hutchinson for the Cleveland County Archaeological Unit).

The Thorpe Thewles farmstead

Like the site at Winnall Down, 400km (248 miles) further south, the Thorpe Thewles farmstead (*Plate 14*) lay within a gated ditch and bank enclosure, this time about 0.75ha (1¾ acres) in size. Like the more southerly site, its interior was divided up into different areas, and there were round buildings scattered about. The same range of animals was kept, although in different proportions; there were more cattle than on the southern chalklands.

One thing that was clear from David Heslop's excavations of the site was that cereals were just as familiar a part of the archaeological debris at Thorpe Thewles as they were on farms further south. Not only were charred grains of spelt wheat and six-row barley found by the thousand, but the site produced numerous fragments of quernstone.

Rotary 'beehive' querns, so called on account of their shape, are found all over the north. They were manufactured from rough-outs quarried in the Pennines and the North York Moors, and then traded across the region. Once again, we can see the strands that link these farmsteads into much wider networks.

The work at Thorpe Thewles shows how, just as in the south of the country, the fertile river basins of the north could support mixed farming settlements, using both stone and metal as well as wood, and using the same crops and animals as in the south.

The north also had its more remote settlements. One hundred kilometres (62 miles) further to the north-west from the rolling boulder clay landscape that supported Thorpe Thewles, the land rises up onto the old, worn slopes of the Cheviots, at the very north of England. The

Cheviot itself rises to 816m (2677ft), and is a landmark on the horizon throughout the north-east. The rivers that cut down the Cheviot slopes, and drain into the Till, the Aln and the Coquet, pass through vast, open landscapes, here and there dotted with the stony remains of settlements occupied in the second and first millennia BC.

Scattered settlement on the Cheviot Hills

To the north of the Cheviot lies the hillfort of Yeavering Bell with over 100 houses within its fortifications. Beyond, the landscape is scattered with sites, a scatter that thins out towards the south, such that each site may be several kilometres from its neighbour.

These remote sites often had only a single round house, leaving a ring of collapsed stone in the modern heath. Alongside these circular traces, a small cluster of fields may be visible, covering little more than 0.5 ha (1¼ acres). They are not the organised parallel field systems of Chapter 5; they are simply piecemeal enclosures, made by throwing stones cleared from the shallow soil to its edge. Elsewhere the stones cleared in this way are merely piled up into cairns, peppered across the landscape.

The pollen evidence from the region seems to suggest a shifting patchwork of clearances on these hillslopes, where isolated farmers attempted to farm this remote region. At one site on Snear Hill, the traces of hand-hoed ridges are visible, suggesting that these farming units may have been too small to maintain a ploughteam.

The general impression is of a wave of pioneer settlers, moving into regions remote from the home range of their forefathers, but no doubt dependent on their distant lineage for social reproduction, much as New World settlers depended on, and maintained links for several generations with their Old World lineages. By the end of prehistory, the north-east was widely settled.

The centuries of Roman occupation saw a similar growth of rural settlement to the west of the Pennines. This was a period when some of the other remaining gaps in the human landscape were filled with rural settlement. The East Anglian Fens at this time became as densely settled as they are today. Countless settlements clustered along each meandering watercourse, grazing their flocks and panning for salt along its misty banks.

PATTERNS THROUGH TIME

The settlements that leave their trace as a scatter of ditches, pits, postholes and the occasional upstanding structure, had life-spans that ranged from a handful of summer seasons, as at Farmoor in the Upper Thames Valley, to the best part of a millennium, as at Winnall Down on the Hampshire chalklands. It was common, as it is today, for a farmstead to remain in use for several centuries, albeit with a fair amount of rebuilding. New farmsteads could become established, grow, decline and disappear for a wide variety of reasons; we can see this happening at different stages on different sites.

Plate 15 Aerial view of a prehistoric farmstead near Great Swinburne in Northumberland. The round houses and farm walls show up clearly within the snow (photo: T. Gates).

There are some periods that seem to see more change than others. The first half of the first millennium BC is one such period, when a substantial number of farmsteads came into existence. The final century of the millennium is another, when a number of changes occur. On the southern chalklands, several of the enclosed farmsteads are broken down into smaller ditched units. This also happens in the Thames Valley where, in addition, seasonal occupation ceases on the floodplain and new rectilinear enclosures appear along the gravel terraces. In the Midlands there is an expansion of new sites into areas dominated by boulder clay, and in the north new sites appear on a range of soil types, while pollen samples provide evidence of unprecedented levels of woodland clearance.

A further period of change comes in the late third and fourth centuries AD. At this time some of the farms with greater material wealth adopted a new range of farming tools, making use of much larger quantities of iron than their predecessors. Alongside the use of their larger sickles, scythes and heavy ploughs, these farmers experimented with new crop repertoires, and have also left traces of carefully dug plots that may belong to our first 'market gardens'.

These periods of marked change are also times of transition for other features of the landscape, and are also evident in relation to the larger sites. The first period is when hillforts develop from large, but simple enclosures to heavily defended, heavily populated centres. The second period is when these hillforts fade in importance, and the centre of activity shifts to the massive, low-lying oppida, located with access to the waterways. They are clearly periods when a pulse of change reverberated through the entire human landscape, affecting large and small settlement alike. We have seen in the previous chapter how such reverberations might find their stimulus in developments on the international scene. In this chapter we can turn from the large to the small scale, and see those reverberations within individual farming settlements.

The changing fates of individual farms

The long-lasting settlements such as Winnall Down, Thorpe Thewles and the Ashville site each underwent marked structural changes through time. At Winnall Down and Thorpe Thewles the enclosed sites were superseded by more open, expansive sites. Developments at the Ashville site were rather different.

We have already seen that this site was largely given over to cereal and sheep farming. It is one of the very many farmsteads that appear in the archaeological record of the middle of the first millennium BC. As soon as the first pits and postholes were dug, the refuse gathering within them included copious evidence of mixed farming. Sheep, cattle, horses, pigs and dogs were kept. Six-row barley and three different types of wheat – spelt, emmer and bread wheat – were in production. A rich weed flora was already in evidence, suggesting that arable plots were well established in the landscape.

During the next few centuries, new round houses and their outbuildings appeared in the core of the settlement, and in the surrounding land, cereal production was pushed onto ever more marginal soils. We can see it being pushed onto damp ground, by the appearance of plants of very damp conditions among the charred weeds. We can follow cultivation onto infertile ground by the increased occurrence of weeds that thrive in soils low in nitrogen. In other words we see a farming unit being pushed to its limit.

Through this period, the round house known best from excavation progressively reduced in size, and actually during the last stages of the millennium, the whole settlement was restructured, and some of the housing plots turned into paddocks. The site continued in this form, and eventually faded in the third century AD. The last scatters of refuse suggest that similar farming methods had been in use throughout the many centuries of the settlement's life. Sheep were still the major animal, and spelt wheat and six-row barley the major crops. As the walls of one of the last farm wells caved in, they sealed and preserved the tip of an ard that had been thrown in. This ard-tip was of a traditional kind, the same kind of implement that had been in use since the farm's inception.

No more than 2km ($1\frac{1}{4}$ miles) from the Ashville site, a different kind of farmstead had appeared. Just as the former settlement was undergoing its greatest change in the final stages of the first millennium BC, so was a small enclosed farmstead set up on a gravel terrace to the west, a site we call Barton Court Farm.

The enclosure around this site contained one or two buildings and a small provision for storage. At the base of a storage pit were the charred remains of an early harvest. As at the Ashville site, sheep, spelt wheat and six-row barley were predominant, but in addition, a large proportion of the cereal remains at Barton Court Farm were of bread wheat, a crop that occurred as no more than a trace at the nearby Ashville site. Bread wheat is the crop we grow today, and is, alongside rice, the major food source of the human species. Sites like Barton Court Farm mark the beginnings of its rise from a minor crop in prehistory to prominence in the historical period.

It seems that as a traditional farm at Ashville went into decline, so its more innovative neighbour flourished. Barton Court Farm went on to incorporate a neighbouring cattle farm on the lower slopes of the valley, and eventually to adopt the fashions and living styles of the Romans who had gained power over the country. By the fourth century AD we see a timber-framed house with mosaic floors, painted walls, and window glass; it had become a villa. It started and continued with innovative agriculture – bread wheat at first, eventually adding flax and beans and spices to its repertoire.

Turning from the biological remains to the material evidence, we can see that from its pre-Roman beginnings, the occupants of Barton Court Farm had used coinage, and this may be significant. Innovation in agriculture, as in other fields, involves access to new ideas, new stocks and new equipment, such as we have seen were becoming available at the time Barton Court Farm was growing. The use of coinage at the new centres that were appearing along the waterways may be a symptom of that access as well as of the power to use it, which farmers in other settlements were denied.

This single example illustrates the point that has recurred throughout this chapter. Looking at the physical evidence alone, we see a pattern of rural settlement in the first millennium that contrasts with that of the preceding period. Dispersed scatters of houses, nested within large-scale systems of land division, are replaced by nucleated clusters of settlement, in hillforts and perhaps in villages, together with a vast number of smaller settlements. Yet although these smaller sites may seem detached from one another in plan, when we examine the biological evidence and consider social and biological reproduction, we see a whole range of interconnections, both between them and with the hillforts and other nucleated settlements in the landscape. It is these interconnections that linked their fate with global social and economic developments.

Such links may also have given rural settlement a flexibility not previously experienced. The link with more versatile exchange systems, with the ability, for example, to acquire iron for utilitarian items, and the access to larger and more fluid gatherings of people, created the conditions where populations could grow, and expand into new areas of the English landscape. The explosion of apparently detached smallholdings across the country in the first millennium BC marked one of the most substantial changes the English landscape had seen. The wildwood may have been diminished by countless previous generations, but in the last centuries of prehistory we see the full switch from clearings within a wildwood, to wooded patches within an open, agricultural landscape. Having explored the settled landscape, we can now return to the woodland to see how it has fared through these many changes.

8

The last of the wildwood

From the earliest farmers and beyond, we can find evidence from pollen of openings in the wildwood, and we can see those openings spread and grow. At the end of prehistory this spread accelerated dramatically. We can follow in the pollen record a wave of woodland diminution starting in the south in the first half of the first millennium BC, engulfing Yorkshire and the Pennines during the course of the millennium, and by the end of the millennium spreading throughout the north-east. In each of these areas the wildwood was already reduced, but none of them had seen the scale of reduction that accompanied the surge of settlers whose footsteps we followed in the previous chapter.

This massive opening up of the wildwood had a marked destabilising effect on the landscape. Topsoil poured off the hillslopes into the neighbouring river valleys, where we can still find it today as thick bands of alluvium sealing the prehistoric sites that lay along the river bank.

The woodland that once surrounded the human landscape, continuously encroaching and repeatedly being pushed back, was to adopt a different place in the environment as perceived by humans. The fragmented woods around the perimeters of agricultural land would become a limited resource, to be protected and carefully managed. They would be seen as sacred places by the druids that Caesar encountered, their great oaks treated with ceremony, and offerings made up to the pools and streams within them.

These are not the same woods that spread back over the glacier-ravaged landscape in previous millennia. Just as the human presence had carved deep into other parts of the landscape, so could their impact be seen in the surviving woodland. In this chapter we explore that impact, which involves not only the obstructive, but also the constructive aspect of woodlands in human life.

WOODLAND AS A COMMODITY

We have seen how a dense growth of woodland impedes animals which, like humans, have a poor sense of smell and so rely heavily on vision. Even as the post-glacial woodland was closing up over the English land surface, we can see attempts being made to open it up again. Yet alongside this negative aspect, it is quite clear that woodland has consistently served as a major resource for humans, not only in terms of

Figure 33 Map of locations
cited in Chapters 8 and 9.

Figure 34 Prehistoric craftsmanship: wooden objects from Glastonbury (adapted from A. Bulleid and H. Grey 1911 *The Glastonbury Lake Village*). *Above*: components of a wooden wheel. *Below left*: axle block. *Below right*: incised wooden bowl.

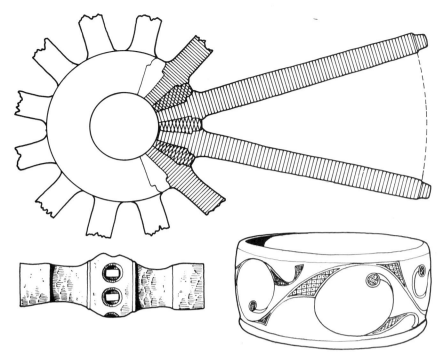

foodstuffs, but also in the enormous diversity of other commodities it offers, for fuel, for the construction of buildings and tools, and for an enormous range of craft activities. A commodity used extensively in all of these is, of course, wood itself.

The age of wood

Prehistory is customarily divided into the ages of stone, bronze and iron, on the basis of contemporary technology reflected in archaeological finds. Were all our sites waterlogged, and were we to have a clear picture of the major technological activities of each age, we would without hesitation lump the entire period discussed in this book into a single age, the age of wood.

At the end of prehistory, we might encounter a family toiling in the field with sickles of iron, but if we turned to look at their ard, hoes, ox yoke and carts, we would see a great deal of wood and very little metal. Back at the homestead, one or two people might be wearing ornaments of bronze, and that might be the only metal in a view made up of wooden houses, wooden fences and a wide variety of structures and implements of wood.

The trees were not only a source of wood, but we can catch no more than a glimpse of the full range of materials derived from trees. Oak bark and oak galls have a long history of use in the tanning of leather. The elder Pliny talks in the first century BC of a trade in oak galls for this purpose. Bast from the lime tree has often been used to make fibres and rope; a strand of rope recovered from the second-millennium BC Wilsford shaft in Wiltshire may have been of this material. On an earlier site at Runnymede on the lower Thames, a sheet of cut bark was found, perforated along the edge so that it could be stitched, perhaps in the making of a boat.

Because so many archaeological sites lack the necessary soil conditions for the survival of wood, it is easy to grossly underestimate its importance relative to the more durable materials. Where those conditions do exist, we see the tip of an iceberg of sophisticated wood technology that must have underpinned prehistoric and medieval life. At Glastonbury in Somerset, for example, the waterlogged soils have preserved a few fragments which testify to that sophistication; alongside a range of commonplace tools we find the spokes and axle-blocks of elegantly crafted wheels. A wooden bowl has been recovered with the same swirling designs that ornament the pottery and metalwork of that period.

Not far from the source of these elegant items lies a great deal more information about early wood technology. The site of Glastonbury overlooks a plain of peat know as the Somerset Levels, and below the peat surface is a remarkable range of structures constructed entirely of wood.

THE SOMERSET LEVELS PROJECT

Since at least the nineteenth century, those who have observed the peat cutting in the flat lands between the Quantock and Mendip hills, have from time to time noticed horizontal bands of wood within the moist black peat. When exposed, these bands can be seen to be wooden trackways linking the drier 'islands' of slightly raised ground and the hillslopes either side of the levels. Sometimes these trackways are formed from a scatter of brushwood, and sometimes they are made up of wattle hurdles or planks.

The Levels attracted the interest of Sir Harry Godwin, a major figure in the development of environmental archaeology. In a pioneering study, he managed to relate the peat deposits and the sediments underlying them to a post-glacial sequence involving not only vegetation succession, but also fluctuating water levels and periodic flooding. It was clear that the peat that was being cut had formed over thousands of years, and that the trackways within it were prehistoric.

The study of these trackways has continued with the work of the Somerset Levels Project, established in 1973. A large number of trackways have been examined, and many of the techniques of environmental archaeology have been applied to the tracks themselves and to the peat around them. Among the various results that have come from its work, the project has provided a unique insight to the early use of wood.

The tracks of the early farmers
Among these tracks is the oldest surviving wooden trackway in the world, the Sweet Track (*Plate 16*), laid down 6000 years ago. It is made

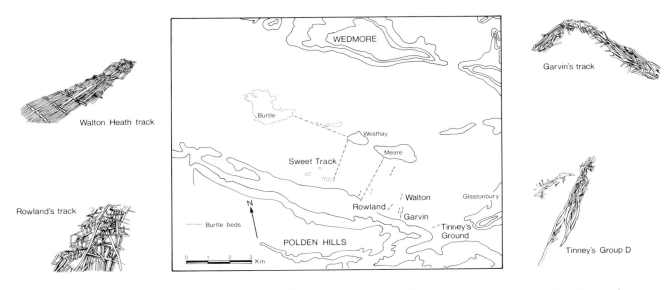

Figure 35 The Somerset Levels: sites and trackways mentioned in the text (adapted from *Somerset Levels Papers*).

up of a combination of pegs, poles and peat packing, which formed a basis upon which oak planks could be lain, providing a narrow walkway across the reedswamp beneath. These planks were made by splitting massive trunks into thin cake-slice segments. An examination of the annual rings on these segments shows that some of the oak trees from which they were made were 400 years old and 1m (3ft) in diameter. They are fragments of that ancient wildwood described in Chapter 2, where the canopies of tall straight trees crowded out the light. These oaks would have been laboriously chopped down with small stone axes, whose marks can still be seen on many of the pieces of wood. No less laborious would have been the task of moving quantities of timber out of the wood onto the swampy levels.

The very ancient trees are the first to reduce in number after extensive felling of a wildwood, and as the life expectancy for trees is foreshortened, so the woodland adopts a generally younger appearance. The form of the trees also changes. From the massive stumps left after a felling episode will spring a cluster of fast growing poles, fed by the reserves of the equally massive rootstocks. These clusters of poles, though a familiar feature of woodland that is regularly cut back, would have been quite unusual in much of the wildwood. Only on unstable slopes where ageing trees fell down themselves and sprouted new growth would this effect have been seen.

Where this regrowth did occur, the long straight poles would have been a very useful form of wood. Indeed there is much evidence of such poles being used in the early trackways. The poles and pegs of the Sweet Track were of this form.

A thousand years on from the construction of the Sweet Track, structures made entirely of this woody regrowth abound and several have been examined within the project. They provide a valuable insight into how wood was being used in the period when massive monuments of earth and stone were being assembled elsewhere in the landscape in honour of the dead.

Early woodland management

Three trackways that date from about 3000 BC, known as Garvin's Track, the Walton Heath Track (*Plate 17*) and Rowland's Track respectively, formed the subject of a detailed study by Oliver Rackham. They were made up of the fast regrowth of hazel, together with some birch and ash. Garvin's Track was made up of armloads of wood thrown down onto the growing peat surface. The other two were more intricate: they were composed of wattle hurdles lain end to end, and the form these pieces of wood took betrayed a great deal about their individual histories.

Many were curved at their bottom end, where they had arisen from

Plate 17 Somerset Levels: the Walton Heath Track, displaying the skilful use of managed underwood in the construction of hurdles (photo: Somerset Levels Project).

the felled stump or 'stool' of the tree. A ragged end reflected how the poles had been cleaved off the stool with stone axes, and sometimes with difficulty. These poles only had a few growth rings, showing that they had grown relatively quickly, and the central growth ring was particularly wide, a characteristic of fast early regrowth from a stool. Further up these poles, the occasional kink corresponded to a side branch. In each case this branch had been removed, and the wound had healed over. In other words the side branches had been lopped off long before the poles had been cut.

The age of the poles ranged between two and 17 years, while their diameters clustered into two groups, one of about 2cm ($\frac{3}{4}$in) and one of about 4cm ($1\frac{1}{2}$in). It seems that these early gatherers of wood moved through the woodlands selecting only that regrowth that was of the right diameter for the job in hand. By continually returning to and cutting the same patch of woodland, they could assure a sustained

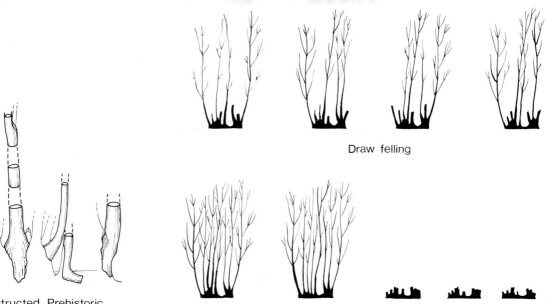

Draw felling

Reconstructed Prehistoric
hazel stool

Plot felling

availability of regrowth from the many felled stumps in the area. The lopped side branches suggest that poles of 'roundwood' were not the only harvest; the leafy branches were also gathered, presumably for fodder.

We can describe this relationship, where some active involvement is taken by the users of wood in its growth and replenishment, as woodland management. The form of management outlined above can be described as draw felling, and the form of woodland it produces as coppice woodland containing continually recut stumps known as coppice stools.

Coppice woodland was a very familiar feature of the landscape in the Middle Ages. Each parish would have access to such a woodland and use it extensively for fuel, timber, and constructional purposes. Such woods had a remarkably neat appearance in comparison with the wildwood. The death and decay so commonplace in the wild wood was more or less absent in coppice woods, as trunks, branches, twigs, bark and leaves were all taken away and put to some use. The difficult journey through a dense wildwood contrasted with the ease of access along medieval woodland rides, and the ancient towering trunks on either side in the wildwood gave a very different impression from the constant spring of fresh young growth from the coppice stools.

We must not imagine, however, that the managed woodlands of the early farmers were identical to those of their medieval forebears over 4000 years later. We know for certain that the form of management was different. In the Middle Ages poles were not harvested by draw felling, but by felling whole plots at once, and returning to fell each plot on a regular basis. So, for example, hazel was frequently coppiced on a seven-year basis.

In some ways this difference between draw felling and plot felling is rather like the difference between grazing on common land and grazing

Figure 36 Forms of coppicing. *Left*: a reconstructed prehistoric coppice stool (after O. Rackham in *Somerset Levels Papers* vol. 4). *Right*: schematic diagram of draw-felling and plot-felling.

within a field of pasture. One involves moving around the landscape selecting suitable grazing spots. The other involves a restriction to a particular area of ground which is then used to the full. In plot felling, all the regrowth within the plot is taken, producing a crop of poles of varying diameters, but all of the same age.

Returning to the Somerset Levels, work on a wide range of trackways of various dates is allowing us to gain some idea of the changes of woodland management through time. Among these changes are some early indications of plot-felling. Just west of Glastonbury, a whole series of brushwood tracks run down from Sharpham Park onto Tinney's Ground on the Levels. They were laid down well over 1000 years after the three tracks discussed above, at a time when much of the open countryside had been divided up by the extensive parallel systems described in Chapter 6. One of these Tinney's Ground trackways, Tinney's A, has been traced for 200m (656ft) of its length. It was constructed first of a series of oak slats, boards and planks, pegged onto the growing peat, and a few years later was refurbished using a large number of alder poles, and twigs and wood scraps as packing.

These alder poles displayed much the same variety of form that the hazel poles from the earlier tracks had shown, such as the curved base of many poles, and the axe marks showing where they had been rent from the coppice stool. A notable difference from those earlier hazel poles was the distribution of age and diameter. The Tinney's Ground alder wood was far more strongly clustered around the mean age of seven to eight years, and more widely dispersed in diameter, than the hazel wood from the earlier tracks. Perhaps we are seeing that, just as the open countryside is being divided up into defined land units in the second millennium BC, so are plots of woodland being allocated to particular groups, and being coppiced in a manner more similar to their medieval successors than their early farming predecessors.

We may be able to see the same thing from another component of managed woodlands. Evenly spaced among the coppice stools of a medieval woodland are the taller 'standard' trees, left to grow up above the coppiced trees. These form a longer term supply of large timbers, to be taken less frequently than the underwood.

At the Meare Heath track, which is broadly contemporary with the tracks on Tinney's Ground, such 'standard' trees may be in evidence. The growth patterns on some of the oaks used for this track show cyclical variations, suggestive of repeated bursts of growth in the more open conditions that follow plot felling of the surrounding trees.

PUTTING THE WOODS TO USE

We may not have the excellent conditions of preservation found on the Somerset Levels on every site, but even when all that remains is a series of ditches, pits, and postholes, the fundamental importance of managed woodland is clear. It is certainly possible to construct a log cabin from cleaved wildwood trunks, and many early dwellings may have been of this form. Yet the whole round house tradition that dominated vernacular architecture for over two thousand years of English prehistory depended on the availability of managed woodlands. Without a source of long, flexible, straight poles, the construction of a conical roof becomes a formidable task. The houses, fences, and out-buildings reconstructed by Peter Reynolds at Butser Hill use managed wood exclusively, and there is every reason to suppose that much the same was true of many prehistoric settlements.

The archaeological record provides other clues as to the use of woodland. The seeds and bones discarded by early farmers show that they were not invariably reliant on agriculture for food. For over 2000 years after the beginnings of agriculture in England, hazelnut shells continue to be one of the commonest seed fragments on archaeological sites, sometimes accompanied by the pips of crab apple.

A similar comment can be made of woodland animals. The bones of wild pigs, wild cattle and deer continue to appear in human settlements long after the earliest farms were created. Even when the consumption of woodland animals declines in the first millennium BC, antler continues to be a much used material. The woods were also used to graze domestic animals, and the best known example is pannage for pigs.

Pigs in the woods

The importance of pigs to humans lies in their ability to turn a remarkable range of materials into a useful combination of protein and fat. Around settlements they were an important means of recycling human waste. In woodlands they provided a mechanism for turning the motley range of unpalatable debris on the woodland floor into food. In the Middle Ages, the practice of putting pigs out in the autumn woods to fatten up on acorns and beech mast was widespread. In the Domesday Book, the woods of a large part of eastern England are quantified in terms of the number of pigs they might support.

Documentation of woodland pannage goes back to the eighth century. Beyond that all we can say is that pig bones are a common, and in some periods the commonest category of bone found on archaeological sites. Looking at the use of pigs in other parts of the world today, it does seem likely that the use of woodland for pannage has considerable antiquity in this country.

It is quite feasible for domestic pigs to be left continuously in a woodland environment, with virtually no human intervention. The minimal contact is to establish a social bond between pig and human, by giving the sows shelter during birth, such that the pigs can eventually be collected together and culled. This minimal form of pig husbandry differs only marginally from pig hunting, and such minimal strategies may have been frequently adopted by early farming groups.

Fuel from the woodland

For almost the entire duration of human history after the discovery of fire, the major fuel was wood. Not only can a fire consume enormous quantities of wood, but that consumption is sustained; a large wooden house may last for years, but the small fires within it must be replenished daily. The gathering of fuel would have constituted one of the main demands placed on early woodlands, and vast areas of coppice woodland would have been created and sustained as a result of fuel gathering alone.

While this would have been true throughout much of prehistory, the effect would have multiplied dramatically as fire was extended from the domestic to the industrial sphere. Considerable quantities of fuel can be consumed in the production of pottery, salt, glass and, in particular, metal.

In the early stages, metal was produced on a relatively small scale, and the early bronze furnaces were no more than a simple bowl about 0.3m (1ft) across. Such bowl furnaces continued in use within settlements as iron became included in the technological repertoire. It was only towards the end of prehistory, and especially during the period of Roman rule, that metal production became a really large-scale activity.

The sheer quantity of iron surviving on Roman sites far outweighs the amount surviving from prehistory, and the size of the slag heaps from iron production in the Roman period can be thousands of times greater than the largest of their prehistoric predecessors. In the Wealden district of Kent and Sussex, we find copious evidence of the burnt clay and ash that survives from their furnaces, and the open-cast quarries from which they dug the iron ore. The production of charcoal to fuel this industry must have placed massive demands on the woodlands of the Weald, but a sustained, well-managed industry would not necessarily have reduced their size.

Henry Cleere has estimated the annual output of the six main Wealden ironworks controlled by the Roman provincial navy to be in the order of 550 tons a year, which would require the charcoal from over 46,000 tons of wood a year. This, in turn, according to Oliver Rackham, could have been continuously supplied from around 100sq. km (38½sq. miles) of coppice woodland.

The sheer scale of Roman construction and manufacture, in particular by the army, would have consumed large quantities of wood in a number of ways, be it as a raw material in the construction of palisades and fortifications and boats, or as a fuel in the production of metal, pottery, bricks and tiles. While this use may have been fairly haphazard during the initial advance of the Roman army, the sustained use that followed would by necessity have involved managing the woods. The effect of Roman industry is consequently more likely to have been evident in the conversion of large tracts of wildwood to managed woodland, rather than in its actual reduction.

This changing character of the woodland did not relate simply to industry, but also to various forms of recreation. Two of the luxuries of Roman life were underfloor heating and hot baths. Both of these, especially bathing, placed extra demands on the woodland as a source of fuel. The wood consumption of a relatively modest suite of Roman baths at Welwyn in Hertfordshire has been estimated at 114 tonnes per year. This would absorb the produce of around 23ha (57 acres) of coppice woodland, and the labour of one woodman. If we multiply this by the hundreds of villas in the country, and add the larger bath complexes in Roman towns, we have a demand on fuel that, while dwarfed by the demands of contemporary industry, is still clearly of some magnitude.

Hunting in the woodland

The villas that possess the most luxurious bath-houses may also be floored with colourful mosaics, depicting many facets of Roman life, including their love of hunting. This aristocratic activity marks a quite new approach to the woodlands and the wild animals within them. Through the course of later prehistory the remains of all wild resources had become progressively less common in archaeological deposits, but during the Roman period, it seems that deer and wild boar were once again sought out, but this time for sport rather than out of necessity.

The emergence of this sporting attitude is reflected in an inscription from County Durham, which records the dedication by a cavalry prefect of an altar to Silvanus, god of the woods, following the capture of a wild boar 'of remarkable fineness which many of his predecessors had been unable to bag'.

The sport of hunting was also a feature of later aristocracies. The Anglo-Saxon kings were fond of the chase, and the place-name Kingswood in the Weald of Kent may well reflect a woodland largely given over to hunting. Woodstock Chase in Oxfordshire, and Brown Clee Hill in Shropshire are two other hunting haunts of the Saxon kings. Although well established by the Anglo-Saxon period, the full impact of the passion for hunting on the landscape was to await the appearance of Norman overlords.

The Norman kings took whole tracts of land outside common law so that they could indulge their love of hunting. At one stage during the twelfth century a third of the English landscape was given over in this way. By no means all of these Royal Forests were wooded, but their existence must have encouraged the spread of woodland, and of the wild animals within them. They would also have encouraged the development of tracts of fairly open land with large trees scattered within them. This 'wood pasture', as it is termed, survives in many of today's parks and forests.

The resurgence of the woodland

The impact of hunting as a sport reminds us of the danger of creating too simple a picture, in which a blanket of wildwood steadily decreases, while what remains is 'tamed' into a storehouse of useful and accessible materials. The open ground and managed woodland of prehistory and history only remained open and managed because of the constant and sustained human usage of them. When that usage lapsed, the ecological process of succession would ensue, and these areas tumble down to woodland once again. A change in land use or a drop in the human population could thus reverse the trend towards an open landscape, and see the English land surface wooded once again.

Several of the pollen diagrams that reflect the decline of woodland also bear witness to its subsequent regeneration. In some periods it seems that regeneration is outstripping woodland removal. Such a period has been noticed around the beginning of the third millennium BC. We can see variation in space as well as time. John Evans' work on the evidence of snails in the Avebury region suggested that an open landscape created by early agriculture was sustained right through prehistory. Yet similar work he conducted around monuments on another part of the chalk downs, the Berkshire Downs, reflected the repeated resurgence of woodland over a less intensively farmed part of the landscape. Only in the first millennium BC did these downs develop an open aspect that was to persist.

The woodland edge

The continued breaking up and reforming of bodies of woodland, and the lesser fluctuations of woodland boundaries, each enhanced the extent of the woodland edge, an ecosystem which proved to be a particularly favourable habitat for a number of animals, including humans.

The woodland edge could be regarded as an intermediate stage in the succession from open ground to full woodland. It is rich in shrubs that bear their foliage within easy reach of the mouths of many woodland grazers. It is also rich in nuts and berries that would attract animals and humans alike. It would bear flushes of bracken, whose rhizomes are a favourite food of pigs. We can therefore imagine pigs, deer and humans all making good use of this transitional ecosystem. While such habitats and the species they favour may have been encouraged by the constant interplay between humans and trees, by the time the Domesday Book was written, the true wildwood had decreased to a small fraction of its former self. In the process, a number of its characteristic components has diminished or disappeared.

Endangered species

One of the earlier species to disappear during the combat between human communities and the wildwood was the elk, which was extinct by the time agriculture reached this country. As we have seen in Chapter 2, however, the demise of the elk is probably best explained in terms of the normal process of woodland succession; in which case the elm tree was the first substantial victim, but nevertheless one which recovered. The millennia after the Elm Decline were to see more drastic reductions. During the second millennium the small-leaved lime dropped from being a major component of the wildwoods of southern England to the unconspicuous component of the English landscape it is today. More severe was the fate of the wild cow or aurochs, whose massive horns form a striking element of some prehistoric bone assemblages, and which in this period sadly went into extinction. The aurochs survived for much longer in continental Europe; Julius Caesar leaves a vivid description after seeing them in the Black Forest:

> in size these are but little inferior to elephants, though in appearance, colour, and form they are bulls. Their strength and their speed are great. They spare neither beasts nor men when they see them. . . . In the expanse of their horns, as well as in form and appearance, they differ much from our oxen.

Some endangered species survived into the first millennium AD. Wolves were sufficiently familiar to generate such place-names as Wolvey, Woolley, Woolmer, Wolborough and Wolsty. St Guthlac in the eighth century apparently knew what a bear looked like, and brown bear claws have been recovered from tenth-century York. However, the bear had probably disappeared from the wild by the time of the Norman Conquest, as had the lynx. Wild pigs had been hunted to extinction by the thirteenth century, and wolves disappeared from England during the sixteenth century.

The final victim of the decline of the wildwood to be mentioned is the 'wild tree' itself. We have already seen how neither the springy poles of a coppice wood nor the stocky spreading trees of wood pasture give a true picture of the lofty, straight, ancient trunks that humans encountered, and which were felled to create the Sweet Track across the Somerset Levels 6000 years ago. The last specimen in the English landscape has long since been felled. Oliver Rackham has suggested that some of the final specimens may still be visible, in the Dominican friary at Gloucester. In the thirteenth century, 82 oaks are recorded as being given for the friary by Henry III; 61 of these were taken from the Forest of Dean, possibly the last place to contain true wildwood.

Some of these timbers are still visible today in the roofs of the friary church choir and cloisters. They are sawn from massive oaks, 0.6m (2ft) across and 15m (50ft) in usable length. It is only by chance they survive at all; the Dominican friary has gone through many changes since its completion. Between the sixteenth and twentieth centuries different parts of it were converted for use as a mansion, as houses and workshops, and as a mineral water factory. In the early 1960s the Ministry of Works took over the site and set to the restoration of the surviving timber structures, incidentally providing a secure resting place for the last of the wildwood.

9

The blasted heath

We have seen how vast tracts of wildwood retreated, to be replaced by landscapes that were cultivated and managed, and we have seen how the material imprint of those who did the cultivating and managing often remains visible in the landscapes of today. Some of the most striking archaeological landscapes are those that spread high onto the moorlands of the north and west; the hut circles, enclosures and reeve systems on Dartmoor; the dykes and cairns on the North Yorkshire Moors. They are a testimony to the early farming communities that once thrived there. Yet one thing is at odds with this picture – many of the soils within those ancient landscapes are now barren.

The stretches of grass and heather between the reeves on Dartmoor are rooted in an acid, nutrient-poor loam that offers little incentive for today's agriculture. Iron and other minerals have been washed down from the topsoil, to form a hard 'pan' lower in the soil profile, impeding drainage and root growth. Such starved soils are also inhospitable to such soil animals as the earthworms, which are so vital in the maintenance of a healthy soil. All in all, these moors today are better suited to the extensive roaming of black-faced sheep, than to the intensive farming settlements they clearly once knew.

The apparent paradox presented by a wealth of settlement evidence in areas of infertile soil is evident right across England's moorlands, from the Scilly Isles and Bodmin Moor in the south-west to the Pennine Range, North York Moors and Cheviot Hills in the north. Environmental evidence from many of these sites has demonstrated that they were not all made up of remote homesteads stranded on a barren heath; they were thriving farms with range of crops and animals. Like the vegetation, the soils of these areas have clearly changed at some stage. In this chapter we explore that change, and attempt to understand how a tract of wildwood, after being opened up to form an agricultural landscape, might go one stage further and turn into barren heathland. We start by examining the most direct way the land can deteriorate, by the loss of its soils from the hillslopes down into the valleys.

SOIL EROSION

The current mismanagement of the world's surviving wildwoods is having dramatic effects on the soils beneath them. As stretches of tropical rain forest are ripped up to be turned into paper, so the soils that were kept in place by an intricate network of tree roots pour into the rivers and the sea. Something not dissimilar may well have happened when openings were created in the English wildwood. Right from the first impingement on the woodlands by post-glacial hunter-gatherers, we can see signs of soil erosion.

In Chapter 3 we saw how at Flixton Carr on the ancient lake of Pickering in Yorkshire, the flint tools of early hunter-gatherers were found together with evidence of fire. At the same level within the peats that were building up in the lake itself, lenses of inwashed mineral sediment were found, presumably corresponding to erosion from the fired ground surface on the neighbouring slopes. Broadly contemporary inwash deposits can be found on the nearby North York Moors, at Kildale and at Ewe Crag Slack, and farther afield at Shippea Hill in Cambridgeshire. It seems that well before farming had become established, the soils in various parts of post-glacial England were showing signs of disturbance as a result of human action.

With the appearance of agriculture, and the increased scale of woodland disturbance, the incidence and extent of soil erosion increased. Not surprisingly, the impact was greatest in the rugged parts of the country, such as the Lake District.

Along the coastal strip beneath the south-west fells of the Lake District, lies a small lake, or tarn, that receives the runoff draining from Black Combe on the fells. The pollen from within Barfield Tarn spans the Elm Decline. We can see the curves for oak and elm drop, just as the curves for grasses and herbs rise, and the appearance of a trace of cereal pollen. In addition we can contrast the different sediments at these levels. Below the level of the Elm Decline, the pollen is concentrated in a dark organic deposit. Above that level, the pollen becomes more thinly dispersed, within a copious pink clay mud. This presumably is the soil that eroded from the neighbouring fells once they had lost the tree cover so vital in holding that soil in place.

Dating the erosion

Soil erosion continued in subsequent millennia, and those sediments that were not washed out to sea accumulated at the bottoms of valleys, where they can be found today. It is not always easy to tell when the sediments were laid down, and thus obtain a timescale for periods of erosion. The simplest way is to search for archaeological material that has become caught up in the sediments, an early site buried by or sitting on a deposit of valley fill, for example.

Martin Bell has closely studied a series of valley fills on the southern chalklands, in areas that were so densely settled in prehistory that the incorporation of archaeological material within the valley fill becomes highly likely. The valley sediments were carefully excavated, and each artefact found was plotted three-dimensionally. In this way some idea of the scale of erosion in different epochs following the appearance of agriculture was established.

During the third and second millennia BC, the infilling of dry valleys was substantial, but it was in the following millennium that much greater quantities of soil began to erode from the hillslopes, this time emptying into the great river systems of England to be redeposited as extensive bands of alluvium.

On the river Arrow in the Severn-Avon system, well over 1m (3ft) of this first-millennium BC alluvium was found to overly a great mass of drifted tree trunks and large branches, preserved by waterlogging. This mass of wood is a direct testimony to the kind of disturbance that increased erosion to such a degree.

The eroded hillslopes

The effect of erosion on the hills that had lost their soil varied. Some bedrocks weathered sufficiently fast for new soils to reform in place of those that had eroded. In many of these places, a new soil formed that differed from its predecessor. Martin Bell's work outlined above illustrates one such case. The lower levels of the fills of these valleys typically had a high content of loess. This silty material is a major component of the seering dust storms in the treeless zone beyond the glaciers. After the glacial retreat from England it seems likely that much of the country south of the most recent ice-sheet was capped with loess, perhaps to a depth of up to 4m (13ft).

This capping has in most places been either greatly thinned or totally removed by subsequent erosion to valleys and to the sea. The soils above

Plate 18 A prehistoric cairnfield on Danby Rigg, North York Moors (photo: A. F. Harding).

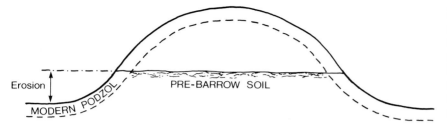

Figure 37 Schematic diagram of a prehistoric barrow in section, showing how past erosion may be inferred from 'perched' buried soils, and how ancient and modern soils may be compared.

these early loess deposits would have been water-retentive and fertile, and in many cases quite different from their successors on the same subsoil.

On the most durable bedrocks, eroded soils would be replaced extremely slowly, if at all. As the soil gradually got thinner and thinner, those stones that were too large to move downhill would accumulate at the soil surface, compounding the poor farmers' problems. We can imagine these farmers wearily hurling the stones to the edge of the plot, where they still remain today, as the clearance cairns scattered around some of our moorland districts (*Plate 18*). Indeed the shift from wood and turf to stone as the constructional material for the Dartmoor reeve systems may also reflect the general trend from moderately deep woodland soils to shallow stony soils.

The archaeological record thus provides us with abundant evidence of soil erosion in prehistory, and some indication of how the new soils that appeared differed from their predecessors. We can explore those differences in more detail by comparing the soils that exist today with those that are buried beneath early structures of earth and stone. These buried soils provide a direct measure of erosion; in many of those that are found on hilltops and hillslopes the level of the buried soil is higher than the adjacent exposed land surface. The difference in height between the two indicates the depth of soil that has eroded since the time the earlier soil was buried.

SOIL PROCESSES

It has already been indicated that erosion is only one of a series of ways in which soils can be modified. Many changes are to the internal structure of the soil. These too can be examined by comparing buried soils with exposed soils; but in order to explore this more fully, we must have a basic idea of how soils work.

The soil is not simply an amalgamation of dirt particles; it is a living and dynamic entity. The actual grains of sand, silt and clay are only one part of a system in which roots, soil animals, micro-organisms, air, water and a whole range of complex chemicals play major roles. The soil is in a constant state of flux; many components are being moved continuously up and down the profile and undergoing various forms of physical, chemical and biological change. As a living and dynamic system, the soil may change its form in response to a multitude of factors. A change in the climate, the vegetation, or the activity of human groups can all modify the soil, for better or for worse.

A good soil is one which is favourable for plant growth. Its structure is such that water and air are available to animals and plants within it. The animals in a soil contribute to its structure by physically mixing it, and recycling and redistributing nutrients and minerals within it. The plants bring biological energy into the soil, and the roots in particular hold the soil together.

At the base of the prehistoric wildwood we would have found a thick layer of rotting vegetation, quickly disintegrating under a welter of insects and bacteria. Beneath this the mineral component would be matted together with a dense network of roots, reaching deep into fissures in the bedrock. These roots would be constantly drawing water and nutrients from the soil, and pumping them up to the foliage above. A thick woodland cover can pump up a volume of water not dissimilar to what comes down again as rain and snow. Nutrients and organic material would be returned to the soil as leaves, branches, and eventually whole trees would fall down on its surface. Here they would be broken down by fungi and insects, and as soluble materials would once again be drawn up through the roots of a new generation of plants.

The efficient cycling of these substances through the ecosystem is crucial to its maintenance, and to the maintenance of the soil that supports it. Unless the vital substances washed down by rain are subsequently pumped back up by the vegetation, then the soil will become depleted, and a new generation of plants and animals will struggle with diminished resources.

Disturbance of the soil system

Two key ways in which these ecological cycles can be disturbed is by an increase in the force of rain carrying substances down, and by a decrease in the pumping strength of the vegetation taking them back up again. Either trend, or a combination of both, can lead to the net movement of substances carried by water downwards through the soil. We can follow this process of leaching by considering the effect of replacing woodland by open ground, and the subsequent decrease in the pumping strength of the more modest stand of vegetation.

As a healthy, well-formed soil begins to suffer from leaching, so the first substances to move down through the soil are those most easily picked up by water. First to move are substances which are readily soluble in water, such as calcium, the basic element of chalk and limestone. Calcium plays an important chemical role in healthy soils. It enables the particles within them to cohere into a crumby tilth, forming a stable basis for plant growth. As the calcium leaches out, so this tilth begins to break down and destabilise. This is the point at which erosion can easily commence.

It is also the point at which particles of clay, no longer held within a stable tilth, can wash down through the soil to reform as a slightly impermeable layer at a lower level. Many of England's modern soils are at this stage, and the evidence from buried soils indicates that soils of this kind had already developed by the time long barrows appeared in the landscape. At Kilham in Yorkshire, for example, a band of washed down clay was visible within the soil buried beneath a long barrow at that site.

The loss of calcium from the surface layers triggers off biological, as well as physical changes. Earthworms and many other soil animals become much less common as the calcium content diminishes and the soil consequently becomes more acid. This means that the soil gets mixed to a much lesser extent, and that there is even more chance of depletion at the soil surface. Bacteria also becomes less plentiful as the soil becomes more acid, and the process of breakdown and decay becomes more dependent on fungi.

An acid fungal leaf mould is quite different from an alkaline bacterial mould. The former breaks down slowly, and the ash-like fragments within it are recognisable as leaf tissue for some time. The latter breaks down fast into a moist, mouldy brown mass. They also release different chemicals into the soil, which in turn influence subsequent patterns of leaching.

One such group of chemicals are known as polyphenols. Once these polyphenols enter the soil, they encourage certain substances, in particular compounds of iron and aluminium, to become mobile and move down through the soil.

Both iron and aluminium are major components of the soil. The reason why so many soils have a reddish or brown colour is the presence of rust-coloured iron compounds within them. As they wash down through the profile of an acid soil, so the upper layers lose their reddish colour and turn to an ashen grey. Further down within the soil the iron and aluminium compounds collect into a rust-coloured 'pan', which can be anything from a thin orange band to a hard concretion, blocking drainage and root growth. Soils in this sorry state are known as podzols, and these are the soils that lie in and around the remains of prehistoric settlement on many English moorlands.

The development of podzols

The iron pans of today's podzols are most easily visible where the Forestry Commission's trenching equipment has ploughed through them, leaving them as jagged fragments of orange concrete scattered across the planting ditches. Where they are intact, we know podzols from the ashen grey leached sediment at their surface, and the covering blanket of heather – a plant well adapted to acid conditions, and whose shallow roots are not thwarted by the impermeable pans.

Heather pollen is known from throughout the post-glacial period, and from the very earliest clearances associated with human activity, its numbers increase markedly. It seems that, following human intrusion, the soil system was in many places quickly rendered sufficiently acid for heather to spread, and this may imply podzolisation. More direct evidence of the podzols themselves comes from Geoffrey Dimbleby's work on soils buried beneath Bronze Age barrows in Yorkshire.

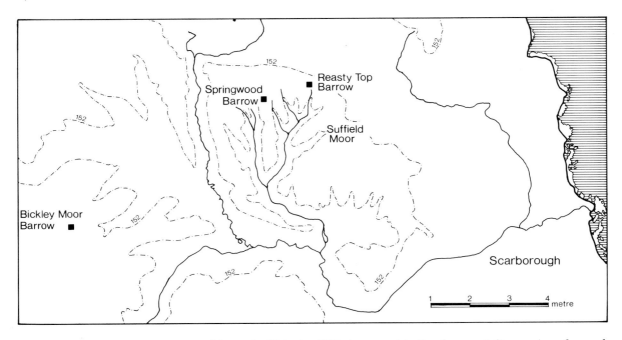

Figure 38 The Tabular Hills, Yorkshire, showing sites mentioned in the text (adapted from G. Dimbleby 1962 *The development of British heathlands and their soils*).

Along the Tabular Hills just outside Scarborough lie a series of round barrows, situated within a heathland landscape of thin soils containing well-developed iron pans. The barrows also bury a range of earlier soils, which often show marked differences from the podzols of today. On two barrows examined from Suffield Moor and Bickley Moor respectively, the modern podzol continued over the top of the barrow, whereas the soils beneath them lacked any sign of an iron pan. At the nearby Springwood Barrow, however, the buried soil was slightly bleached, an early stage in the progress towards podzolisation. At Reasby Top Barrow, the buried soil was at a further stage along this path, and an iron pan was visible. These barrows had incidentally documented the progressive deterioration of soils and spread of heathland in the landscape in which they were erected.

By the end of prehistory, England's modern heathlands had been created, and we can see concentrations of settlement in many places give way to less intensive forms of land use. The heathlands had spread far more extensively in the north and west than in the south and east, reflecting a number of differences between these regions.

The bedrocks of the north and west are generally older, and frequently harder than their counterparts in the south and east. As the soil deteriorates and erodes over these bedrocks, it is not possible to replenish basic elements such as calcium by ploughing into them. They instead remain as durable and inert surfaces approaching closer and closer to the plants growing and animals grazing on their ever more impoverished soils. The second difference is the greater rainfall experienced in the north and west, such that the downward movement of water within the soil is greater. Thirdly the north and west include several areas of rugged topography, where the danger of soil erosion is greater.

The Lowland and Highland Zones

These differences between the south and east, and the north and west, have led to the distinction between the Lowland and Highland Zones, with the dividing line running along the Jurassic ridge from Lincoln in the north-east to Lyme Bay in the south-west. In later prehistory the Lowland Zone was seen as the bread basket of England, with an emphasis on grain production and the rearing of sheep, while the Highland Zone was seen as an area of wandering pastoralists, moving their herds across a bleak landscape.

We can now see that this picture is too simple. England's landscape is a complex mosaic of interdigitating hills and valleys, and that complexity is reflected by the diversity in the ecological patterning within it, and the diversity of human settlement, and human response to that patterning.

In broad terms, however, it is still useful to contrast the lowland and highland areas in terms of the response of their soils to the pressures of human disturbance and climate. In both areas soils on the slopes have deteriorated and been lost into the valleys, but they have differed in the quality of soils that have regenerated in their place. Cultivation of the soft limestone hills of the south and east has led to the formation of shallow, but base-rich soils that continue to support intensive agriculture today. Many of the hillslope soils of highland areas fail to be replenished in this way, and simply get poorer and thinner. They support vast stretches of podzolic soils, and in places are capped by peat.

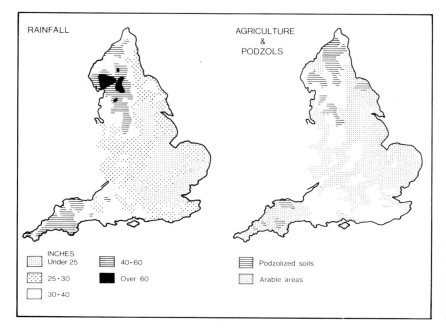

Figure 39 Modern distribution of rainfall, modern podzols, and recent arable land in England (adapted from L. Stamp & S. Beaver 1971 *The British Isles: a geographic and economic survey*).

The spread of peat

This brings us full circle to the deposit that has preserved so much of the evidence with which we can reconstruct early landscapes. We saw at the outset of this book how the deposition of peat represents an extreme along a trend of ever-diminishing rates of biological decay. Peat can be thought of as a kind of backlog of undecayed organic material, piling up on the surface of the land. It is frequently made up of the plant that both thrives on, and helps to spread peat growth, *Sphagnum* moss.

The spread of peat is triggered by changes in rainfall, surface water conditions and run off. Prior to the Elm Decline, fresh growths of peat on the highest ground can be linked with periods of increased rainfall. Peat begins to grow in many parts of the Pennines directly over scatters of chipped flint left by hunter-gatherers eight or nine millennia ago, and it may be that their hunting activities had some part in the initiation of peat growth, though this is hard to prove.

The activities of early farmers clearly had such an effect. From the Lake District to the moors of the south-west there are several instances of peat initiation at around the time of the Elm Decline. In these examples it seems that the reduction of the wildwood influenced the patterns of groundwater, such that peat was able to spread.

It is not difficult to see how this could happen; we can see similar phenomena accompanying modern woodland clearance. The woodland trees not only recycle water, they act as a buffer against the variations in strength and frequency of rainfall. The leafy canopies moderate the impact of a heavy storm at the soil surface, and the roots hold the rainwater when it reaches the ground. The humidity within the sheltered trunk space is also buffered against extremes of rain and sun.

With the canopy removed, this buffer is lost, and the ground surface is at times exposed to extreme wetness. It is then that conditions are ideal for *Sphagnum* peat to spread across the surface, smothering what plants remain, including the ancient tree-stumps still visible in moorland bogs today, and sustaining the waterlogged conditions with its sponge-like tissue. Such peat can form blankets across hillslopes and domed bogs on the high moors. At their centres they may be many metres deep, having grown over thousands of years, trapping and preserving the contemporary pollen rain on the way.

The forces of 'man' and 'nature'

We have seen how human action and climatic change can affect the soil system in similar ways; both can lead to an imbalance between the relative quantities of water and contained substances moving downwards and upwards through the soil. Since the evidence we have of past changes is in the form of the end products of such an imbalance – eroded sediments, deteriorated soils, peat growth and so on – it can be very difficult to tell which of these two agencies is responsible for the change.

As far as climate is concerned, there are several ways in which we can obtain an independent measure of past temperatures, but the effects of increased rainfall are too easily simulated by human disturbance. We may be able to get an independent measure of human activity in the form of settlement evidence, but we have seen how, for some periods, such evidence is remarkably elusive.

To some extent the difficulties of disentangling 'man' and 'nature' reflect the artificiality of the distinction between the two. In taking an ecological approach, the focus of our attention is not the individual components of an ecosystem, but the many *interactions* between them. In this sense it is as unrealistic to ask whether humans rather than 'natural forces' were responsible for heathland formation, as it is to ask whether birch trees rather than 'natural forces' were responsible for woodland regeneration. All components of an ecosystem interact, and it is that series of interactions that moulds the structure of the ecosystem. The absence of any particular component would lead to a different chain of interactions, and consequently a different ecosystem. With that in mind, we can move to a wider context to explore the involvement of humans within the post-glacial landscape of which they have been part.

ENGLAND'S CHANGED LANDSCAPE IN A WIDER CONTEXT

In Chapter 2 we tried to establish an environmental 'baseline' for the human landscape that developed in the post-glacial period. The model we constructed was of a series of shifting zones, each bearing its own ecological pyramid, fluctuating back and forth along with changes in global temperature, advancing and retreating both in latitude and altitude. Within each zone, and within the constraints of climate and soil formation in that zone, the ecological pyramid would tend to maximise its productivity and diversity.

So in the harsh conditions to the immediate south of the glacial belt, the relatively simple tundra ecosystem will form. As we move south to more amenable climatic conditions, it will give way to increasingly diverse woodland ecosystems. As rainfall rather than temperature becomes a limiting factor, further to the south and east of Europe, so simpler ecosystems will once again appear, moving from woodland to steppe, and from there to desert.

If we consider this pattern around 8000 years ago, open tundra-like ecosystems would have retreated to Scandinavia, and to high altitude sites throughout Europe, and coniferous woodland would have spread across the colder regions of the north and the seasonally drier Mediterranean lowlands. Elsewhere the European lowlands would be under a variety of deciduous woodland ecosystems, perhaps bordering on steppe in the Hungarian Plain. Towards the Middle and Near East the increasing dryness would be reflected in the expanse of steppe and desert.

By this period, the earliest farming communities had begun to move along the European waterways, bringing with them plants and animals ultimately derived from the Near Eastern steppe. By opening up the valley woodlands, and implanting these alien species, they were in a sense creating a steppe-like ecosystem in place of a woodland ecosystem. Indeed the primary steppe of the Near East does in many places bear a resemblance to fields of cereals and grassland.

As this steppe-like agricultural ecosystem spread and engulfed much of Europe and the Mediterranean, so on the southern and eastern fringes, the grazing of domestic animals pushed the boundary of the desert ecosystem northwards. If we think of the treeless heathlands discussed in this chapter as tundra-like ecosystems, then we can see a similar thing happening on the northern and western fringes of Europe. The use of domestic plants and animals has pushed the boundary of tundra-like ecosystems southwards.

Putting these trends together, we can create a simplified picture of the human influence on the landscape in terms of shifting the boundaries between different ecological pyramids. In the case of Europe and the Mediterranean, the diverse woodland pyramids in the lowlands of the core have given way to the simpler pyramids derived from the periphery, from desert, steppe and tundra. The net effect on the English land surface has been the shrinkage of ecosystems derived from the wildwood, and the expansion of the steppe-like agricultural ecosystem, and tundra-like heathland ecosystem.

This simple picture can be expressed by the phrase, humans have a simplifying effect on ecosystems; and this phrase certainly captures the destruction of diversity that currently typifies human action within the environment. But we must be cautious of simple pictures; a closer scrutiny of the evidence that environmental archaeology gives us is not consistent with an ever-decreasing ecological diversity resulting from human action. The pattern is more complex than this.

Human action and ecological diversity
The clearest example of the human reduction of ecological diversity is a stand of modern cereals. With an intensive application of chemicals, hectare upon hectare may contain a single variety of a single species, where once several varieties of thousands of species lived. While not all are as extreme as this, many of today's environments contain far fewer species than they might have done in the absence of such human intervention.

Yet the evidence of pollen, seeds and animal remains suggests that some aspects of past human intervention have actually enhanced ecological diversity. So the mosaic of clearance and regeneration encouraged by grazing and fire in the post-glacial wildwood actually expanded the range of plants and animals that can thrive within an otherwise dark, dank interior. In a later period of woodland development, human intervention in the form of coppice management was to stimulate the development of the rich ground floras we still associate with ancient woodland today. The spread of hedgerows across the landscape further stimulated diversity.

Between those hedges, the cultivated fields have not always been dominated by monoculture. Over the millennia numerous species from the original homeland of cereals in the Near East, from the river banks along which early farmers travelled, from woodland edges and naturally disturbed habitats on slopesides and along coasts, gathered together to form the weeds of the field. The numbers of agricultural weeds known from the archaeological record continue to increase throughout prehistory. The routes opened up and used by humans could also be used in the dispersal of plants and animals that could tolerate human activity. We see this most clearly in the range of plants and animals that collect where humans gathered together in early towns.

There is, of course, another side to the story. We have seen in the last chapter the steady decline of species of the wildwood, and we can in a similar way follow the depletion of fish populations in our medieval rivers. The main topic of this chapter, the formation of heathlands, gives us another example of a species-poor ecosystem encouraged by human action.

The overall picture has a variety of elements rather than a single direction. At different places, and at different times, ecological diversity has been both enhanced and reduced by human action, and the current strength of emphasis on reduction is a very recent phenomenon. By the end of prehistory, human activity within the landscape had in some places created species-rich coppice woodlands and hedgerows, meadows and fields with a wide variety of cultivated and wild herbs, and settlements around which a great number of birds, rodents and invertebrates gathered. In other places, however, that same human activity had left former settlements stranded within a species-poor, wind-blasted heath.

10

The emergence of
a Domesday landscape

Not even at the present day are the cities of our country inhabited as formerly; deserted and dismantled, they lie neglected until now, because, although wars with foreigners have ceased, domestic wars continue.

So wrote a sixth-century British cleric named Gildas. He was writing of the aftermath of a major battle at a site known as Mons Badonicus. At this battle, the advance of the colonising Saxons had been halted by a group of Britons under the leadership of a man who would later be identified as King Arthur.

Gildas was writing in the middle of a millennium that has left us countless records of raids, battles and movements of people. In one of the earliest accounts of these islands, Julius Caesar writes of the raiding and settlement of maritime England by invaders from Belgium. Just over a thousand years later, the Domesday Book preserves ample evidence of the ravages inflicted on northern England during the Norman invasion. In between times, parts of the country had been successively overrun by Romans, Germanic groups, and Vikings, and as Gildas suggests, internal conflicts were not uncommon.

We might expect these events to be so disruptive that the human landscape would emerge from the battering in a completely new form after millennia of prehistoric evolution. Indeed the evidence of English place names might easily give this impression; alongside several thousand names that have Anglo-Saxon or Scandinavian roots, those that have Roman or Celtic roots number no more than a few hundred. Yet in trying to understand how the human landscape has evolved in the long term, we must be very careful how we treat the wealth of documentary evidence that appears towards the end of our period of study. While it provides details of some aspects of the landscape with crystal clarity, the evidence from documentary sources, just as much as archaeological evidence, constitutes a highly selective database. Each written record was created with some purpose in mind, and there may be more purpose in recording a change, a dispute, or an upheaval, than recording that the mundane aspects of life were much the same this year as they were last year. Each author may also have chosen to place widely varying emphases on different aspects of observed events. While written records provide a great deal of information about invasion, migration and turmoil in the first millennium AD, it is very difficult to quantify

Figure 40 Map of locations
cited in Chapter 10.

these episodes in terms of numbers of people, and the effect they had on the structure of the human landscape we have been examining.

One approach we can take is to put the historic picture to one side for a moment, and tackle the first millennium AD with the same techniques of archaeology that we have seen applied in prehistory. This we can do by focusing on one of the pioneering projects of medieval archaeology.

WHARRAM PERCY: THE EMERGENCE OF A MEDIEVAL VILLAGE

Sheltering in a steep, grassy valley that dissects the Yorkshire Wolds, stands a small, solitary church, its tower derelict and its roof gone. Looking upstream from the church, the river is dammed up behind an overgrown bank. Downstream, the only other building in sight is the vicarage that served the church until its last service less than half a century ago. The village that went with the church has been gone much longer; its only remains are humps and bumps in the surrounding turf, the vestiges of collapsed buildings and intervening paths and lanes.

Wharram Percy is a good example of a deserted medieval village (*Plate 19*), and such DMV's can be found throughout the country. They were deserted at various times for various reasons. Some became empty at the time of the Black Death; others, like Wharram Percy, were evacuated to make way for a different use of the land.

Because they are deserted, they can be excavated extensively, and as such are the stuff of medieval archaeology. This young branch of archaeology has grown up in the few decades that have passed since that last service was held at Wharram Percy, soon after which excavations began of what remained of the village. Over 30 years later, the results of

Plate 19 Aerial view of the deserted medieval village of Wharram Percy, North Yorkshire. In the top left-hand corner of the picture, the church of St Martin's and its vicarage can be seen nestling in the steep-sided valley. Around the vicarage, and towards the bottom right-hand corner of the picture, archaeological trenches are in view (photo: RCHME).

excavation and survey at Wharram Percy have contributed to changing our view of how England's medieval landscape came into being.

The excavations gradually pushed the development of the site back beyond its earliest record in the Domesday Book. Fragments of Saxon pottery were found here and there, and excavations of the church revealed its Saxon foundations. The original dam was a seventh- or eighth-century wooden structure. This much was not surprising, but these were not the earliest features recovered.

Fragments of Roman pottery were found in a number of places, including a few stretches of ditch and bank of the Roman period. As these traces of early ditch and bank gradually came to light, so the true

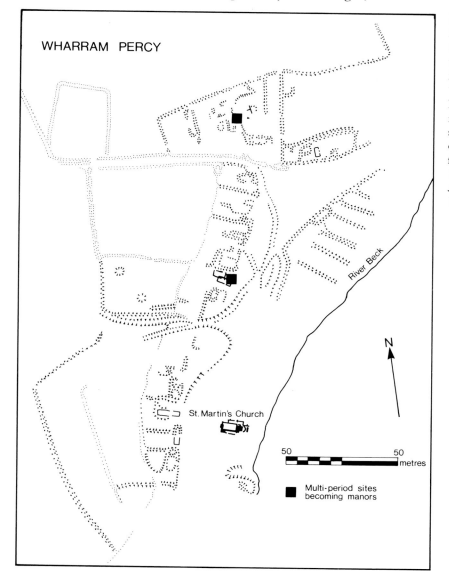

Figure 41 Wharram Percy, indicating the continuity of settlement structure through time. The dotted lines indicate the Romano-British 'skeleton' of the site. The hatched lines indicate the medieval development of the site as survives in the form of earthworks. (Adapted from J. G. Hurst 1979 *Wharram Percy; a study of settlement in the Yorkshire Wolds*).

pattern of Wharram Percy's development became clear. It was not a village laid out anew by early medieval colonists; within the layout of its streets, plots and houses we can see a pattern that was already in existence in the Roman period.

As we scale the slope to the west of the church, to reach the heart of the deserted village, we find a grassy brow crossed by holloways, with the traces of buildings and plots on either side. We can walk along a holloway that was a lane in the fifteenth century, in the Norman period, in the Saxon period, and in the preceding Roman period. The lane bends round alongside the site of a medieval manorial enclosure. This enclosure also contained an Anglo-Saxon site, a Roman period farmstead, and a substantial farmstead of the pre-Roman Iron Age. Just less than 200m (656ft) to the south lies a second manorial complex, also occupied in the preceding Anglo-Saxon and Roman periods. In a millennium of turmoil, in a part of England reached and overrun by Romans, Anglo-Saxons and Vikings, it appears that this little settlement in the Yorkshire Wolds retained a remarkably stable layout.

Few medieval villages have been studied in as much detail as Wharram Percy, but it seems unlikely that its long life-span is unusual. Pottery of late Iron Age and Roman date has been found beneath numerous villages and farmsteads that had previously been assumed to have Anglo-Saxon origins.

Yet it would be wrong to assume that human settlement invariably showed such continuity. Just as Wharram Percy was evacuated in the fifteenth century for motives particular to one area, so in every century some settlements disappeared and others became established. In addition to this general flux of settlement, there were clearly periods in which large numbers of similar settlements underwent considerable adjustment. Such is the case with the smart country houses, or villas that became particularly widespread in the later stages of Roman rule.

THE DECLINE OF VILLAS

These country houses adopted architectural styles drawn from the heart of the Empire: mosaic floors, painted walls, underfloor heating and baths. They varied between extravagant winged buildings and pretentious bungalows, in each case forming the centre of a farming and sometimes industrial unit of equivalent size. It is to these symbols of Roman taste and culture that the upwardly mobile would aspire, and which also played a substantial part in the appearance of the English landscape in the period of Roman rule. However, within a few decades of the departure of the Roman army, a large number of these villas had been abandoned. None remained in use beyond the sixth century.

Like the major Roman towns, these country houses were too bound up with the workings of the imperial machine to survive long without it. Yet as their painted wall-plaster peeled, and the frost and rain got beneath their roof tiles, it seems that the landscapes around them may have lost rather less of their forms.

A number of abandoned villas have Anglo-Saxon settlement nearby. The evidence may be in the form of inhumations; some villa ruins were clearly used as small burial grounds. Such is the case at the villa at Barton Court Farm in Oxfordshire where, in addition to pagan Saxon burials within the ruins, excavation was sufficiently extensive to reveal traces of Saxon huts nearby, whose occupants still made use of the villa's paddocks and yards.

There are several possible reasons why these new occupants chose to live near to, rather than within these villas. They may have had no interest in the particular form of architectural opulence expressed in such buildings. They may have found them uncomfortable to live in or too much trouble to maintain. Whatever the reason, there is a growing body of evidence that this change at the settlement nucleus was not always accompanied by a change in the land unit of which it was part.

THE STABILITY OF LAND UNITS

This contrast between the fates of the settlement core, and the land units of which they were part is well illustrated by Peter Fowler's fieldwork in the Vale of Wrington in south Avon, lying directly north of the Mendip Hills. Evenly spaced along the valley bottom, in some cases together with their surrounding fields, are the traces of some eight or nine villas. In places, this Roman landscape retains traces of its Iron Age forerunner, and the valley is overlooked by the prehistoric hillfort at Cadbury Congressbury.

It was to the safety of this hillfort that the inhabitants of the Vale of Wrington returned, at some time after the villas had gone into decline in the fourth century. They occupied this fort, just as others reoccupied other hillforts in the west of England, during the period of conflict refered to by Gildas at the start of this chapter.

From the seventh century onwards, we can draw on the wealth of written records in the form of charters delineating the boundaries of early estates in the English landscape. A remarkable point about these charters that exist for the Vale of Wrington is that each estate contains the site of one of the earlier Roman villas. We are led to suspect that through the turmoil of the first millennium, settlement may have shifted, but the land units corresponding to Roman villa estates emerged, several centuries later, as Saxon estates. This continuity may also be reflected in some of the minor boundaries. Beneath one of the villas at Lye Hole, the lynchets of a group of the villa's field stretch out. The pattern of these Roman fields is perpetuated in many places by the modern hedge boundaries.

We can find this continuity in the layout of the landscape in many places. Numerous medieval parishes follow the lines of Roman roads, for example along Watling Street in Northamptonshire and Akeman Street in Oxfordshire. In other places, such as at Great Bourton in Oxfordshire, the headlands of medieval fields follow the line of field boundaries of Roman or prehistoric date.

In the north of England, Glanville Jones has discerned the existence of 'multiple estates', in which several townships paid dues to a single territorial lord. These estates, as well as lending structure to the medieval shires, could also be tentatively traced to Roman, or even to prehistoric roots.

Links to such ancient traditions of land demarcation have also been traced by Desmond Bonney in Wiltshire. We saw in Chapter 4 how early farming communities may have marked out their landscapes in relation to monuments to their dead. In the medieval period we see these same long and round barrows followed by the boundaries of Saxon estates (*Plate 20*) and ecclesiastical parishes. In the Stonehenge region alone this applies to at least 40 barrows. The clearest example lies just south of Stonehenge itself, where the parish of Wilsford cum Lake is bounded on the north and west by barrow cemeteries that developed during the third and second millennia BC, and the boundary takes a sharp turn alongside a third barrow cemetery of similar antiquity that lies to the south. The continued symbolic presence of these barrows in the landscape is further emphasised by the addition of at least one pagan Saxon burial within the barrow groups.

The Stonehenge region is not unique in this respect; several Saxon estate charters refer to burials and barrows. Ten such charters for Wiltshire, eight for Berkshire, seven for Hampshire and one for Dorset refer specifically to heathen burials.

The archaeological evidence outlined above shows that there was a great deal of continuity within the landscape of the first millennium AD, especially in terms of the units into which the land was divided. With this in mind, we can return to the documentary evidence, and how it could best be understood in terms of the landscape to which it relates.

Charters and place names

Some 1500 charters defining the boundaries of land-holdings survive from before the Norman Conquest. The earliest known examples are seventh-century in date, but relatively few are known from prior to the ninth century. The earliest of these charters are relatively unspecific about the boundaries concerned, with vague references to nearby natural features, for example. Sometimes bounds are described as 'ancient, and known by the natives', hinting at the continuity we see from the archaeological record.

Through time the boundaries are described in more detail, and charters of the tenth and eleventh centuries are quite specific about the minutiae of the contemporary landscape, providing us with some fine detail of the form it took. In many cases it is possible to trace out these circuit descriptions in today's landscape; a remarkable number of relatively minor features, such as stretches of ditch and small woods, survive.

Margaret Gelling has argued that the increase in detail seen in these boundary descriptions through time reflects the greater number of transactions and disputes over the holding of land. This in turn ties in

with the suggestion made by Peter Sawyer that the appearance of a large number of place names that contain Anglo-Saxon or Scandinavian personal name elements relates, not to pioneer settlement, but to a change in the control over land. So a village called Grimston would no more be created by a Viking named Grimr than Wharram Percy was created by a Norman lord named Percy. In each case the name would relate to a family that had gained control over a pre-existing site.

This picture enables us to draw together the archaeological and historical views of landscape development. By the end of prehistory, much of the landscape had already been divided into recognised units. The upheavals of the first millennium BC saw a great deal of flux in the control of those units, and this is reflected in the proliferation of boundary charters and new place names. Nevertheless, through the course of these upheavals, much of the actual structure of those land units remained intact. This does not of course mean that no new units were created. Nor does it mean that the form the landscape took within the established land divisions remained equally constant. We have already seen how the settlement nuclei within them could change. The cornfields, woods and grasslands around them might also have changed. To explore this further we must turn to the evidence of pollen analysis.

Plate 20 Aerial view of a linear barrow cemetery at Winterbourne Stoke, Wiltshire. The construction of the various barrows spans many centuries in prehistory, and in the historic period their alignment becomes part of a Saxon charter boundary, and subsequently the western limit of the modern parish of Wilsford cum Lake (photo: RCHME).

The pollen record of the first millennium AD
The wave of intensive woodland clearance that had spread northwards

through the country during the previous five centuries finally engulfed the north-western region in the first half of the first millennium AD. A number of pollen diagrams reflect a strong shift towards agriculture at some stage above this clearance horizon, and this has been taken to suggest that bands of colonists were bringing their crops to the marginal areas in the vicinity of peat bogs and tarns. A similar thing might be inferred from the pollen evidence collected from a mere at Old Buckenham in Norfolk, where pollen from rye, flax and hemp appears in the upper part of the diagram at a period that might be linked with Anglo-Saxon colonists.

These particular pollen sequences have a major shortcoming: their fine dating is based on speculation. It is too easy to 'match' the fluctuations with preconceived ideas about how the landscape was forming. More recent pollen sequences have been extensively dated by the radiocarbon method, and they tell a more complex story. A recent pollen sequence from a mere at Hockham, a few kilometres to the west of Old Buckenham, was dated by a series of 13 radiocarbon estimates, and consequently gave a sharper picture of vegetation change. It indicated that during the first third of the first millennium, while the woodland cover stayed much the same, pastoralism gave way to arable farming. In the course of the second third of the millennium, this trend was reversed with pastoralism becoming more prominent. During the seventh and eighth centuries, there was a considerable switch back to arable farming, after which there was a slight reduction of farming activities in general.

This complexity is reflected in other parts of the country for which well-dated pollen sequences exist. Paul Waton's analyses of pollen from around the southern chalklands come into this category. At Amberley, below the South Downs scarp in Sussex, a substantial woodland regeneration early in the millennium is followed by an equally substantial clearance later in the millennium. At Snelsmore on the Berkshire Downs a similar regeneration is not reversed until well into the second millennium. A sequence from just outside Winchester shows a peak of cultivation continuing throughout the millennium, while the same period at Rimsmoor, south of the Dorset Ridgeway, is marked by an erratic pattern of clearance and woodland regeneration.

This first-millennium landscape seems to have been a patchwork subject to different trends in different places. The same is true in County Durham where another series of well-dated pollen sequences exists. Around some sites the agricultural activity established in late prehistory continued through the first millennium; around others it declined after the end of Roman rule, and around others it started afresh.

It seems that as England was subject to different periods of invasion and settlement, so there was a corresponding interchange between stretches of arable land, grassland and woodland. In addition to this, we can make the broad generalisation that these fluctuations were minor in comparison to the wholesale opening up of the landscape in the previous millennium. The general open character of the landscape was already established before the first millennium was underway.

From the varied picture provided by pollen of the first-millennium landscape, we can move to the equally varied picture provided by the text from which this book's title is taken. The classical authors had made fleeting references to aspects of England's landscape. Place names and Anglo-Saxon charters and law codes have provided several clues about woods, trees, farms and fields; but none has the scale or thoroughness of that massive catalogue compiled at the request of William I.

THE DOMESDAY BOOK AS A LANDSCAPE RECORD

The first point to make is that, whatever the true purpose of the Domesday Book, be it a fiscal document, a register of estates, or whatever, it was not compiled for the benefit of students of the English landscape. As King William's commissioners listened to each account of each windswept Pennine valley, they would have been little concerned with the state of heathland development or soil deterioration on the moors above them. As soon as they had compiled a passable valuation of the pitiful valley settlements their king's armies had so recently devastated, they would not have been moved to linger on the details of sad landscapes such as these.

The commissioners' brief was to record the name and extent of each manor or estate in their district, its value and the name of its owner, both at the time of the survey and in the reign of King Edward the Confessor 20 years earlier, the number of tenants, their status and the size of their holdings, and the size of the lord's desmesne. They had also to assess the extent of woodland, meadow, arable and pasture, and record such things as mills, fisheries, salterns and vineyards. It is from this latter group of assessments and records that an impression of the eleventh-century landscape may be gained.

This impression is incomplete in various ways; several features of the landscape fell outside the commissioners' brief, and several that lay inside their brief were clearly missed. We now know that the comment recorded in the Anglo-Saxon Chronicle, 'nor was there an ox, or a cow, or a pig passed by, that was not set down in the accounts', grossly over-estimated the commissioners' thoroughness. It has been suggested that a substantial proportion of the population and up to 20 per cent of contemporary settlements in the survey area were missed.

The Domesday Book, nevertheless, represents a unique and astonishing achievement, and a wealth of information for several aspects of England's past. A central figure in the use of the text in the study of the English landscape is H. C. Darby, who has combed the entire work, and attempted a collation of all the measures of land under different uses. Various difficulties presented themselves, in particular the use of different units of measurement by different commissioners, but the compilation resulting from years of work has provided an invaluable image of the character of the English landscape in the eleventh century. With Darby's work as a basis, we can consider each aspect of that image in turn, in the light of the long evolution of the English landscape discussed in the earlier chapters of this book.

The spread of population

The highest densities of population were along the Sussex coast and in East Anglia and parts of Lincolnshire. The densities gradually fell off towards the north and west, in part reflecting the heath-clad uplands, such as the Pennines and Dartmoor, whose development was discussed in Chapter 9. Low populations are also recorded within low-lying sands, marshes and fenland districts, and on the heavy London clay and Wealden district. This does not mean these areas were not in use; they would, amongst other resources, have provided valuable pasture, and the Wealden woods are known to have been divided up into 'denns' for the pannage of the settlements on its fringe. In addition, the distribution of eleventh-century churches in Kent suggests that there was far more going on in the Wealden district than the Domesday Book betrays.

Outside these areas, the landscape was packed with settlements of various sizes, from the individual 'berewicks', or farmsteads, to the larger 'burhs' or administrative towns. By far the commonest unit of settlement was the 'vill'.

The vill and its ploughlands

Around 13,000 vills are mentioned in the survey. It is clear from the names of many that they correspond to our modern villages, but it is not easy to determine how similar they were in structure to villages of today. By the thirteenth or fourteenth century we can talk of a 'typical' village, nucleated around the village green and encompassed by its open fields, worked in common and cultivated in strips by an eight-oxen team pulling a heavy plough. The Domesday Book provides little clue as to how well developed this unit of feudal society had become two or three centuries earlier. Only in a single entry is there any hint of the existence of open fields divided up into strips and worked in common; in Garsington in Oxfordshire a reference is made to 'one hide of inland which never paid the geld lying scattered among the king's land'. Several Anglo-Saxon charters refer to the physical features of open fields, such as headlands, fore-earths and gores, but we must remember that these relate not to the open field system of tenure, but simply to the agricultural methods used within them.

These methods entail the use, in addition to barley, of crops such as bread wheat and rye, the use of heavy ploughs, which sometimes had to be shared by groups of families, and the heavier soils to which bread wheat in particular is suited. As we saw in Chapter 7, these trends can be traced back to the final years before the Roman Conquest, and so this particular aspect of the workings of the medieval vill is rooted in prehistory. Although the use of heavy ploughing equipment and large ox-teams may in itself imply the communal use of resources, we cannot yet go further to say when or how the organisational aspects of the medieval open field system developed.

One rather surprising observation that can be made is that the extent of cultivated land recorded in the Domesday Book does not appear to have been dissimilar to its extent in the earlier twentieth century. Working backwards in time with the results of environmental archaeology, this in turn reflects on the massive scale that agriculture had reached by the end of prehistory, when the greatest expansion took place.

Such extensive cultivation must have placed considerable demands on domestic animals, both as the major source of power for cultivation and as a source of manure for fertility. Not surprisingly, the Domesday Book records an intensive use of the rich riverside meadows.

Meadows, mills and fisheries

The Domesday survey indicated that the rivers had been put to many purposes. We know little of the antiquity of the numerous fisheries recorded, something that a more rigorous search for fish bones on archaeological sites would remedy. Water mills first appeared with the Roman military installations in England. Fragments of one of these early water mills can be seen at the museum at Chesters on Hadrian's Wall. The rich river meadows we know more of, from archaeological sites like Farmoor on the Thames, discussed in Chapter 7.

This stretch of Upper Thames floodplain had been rich, open grassland for at least 1500 years prior to the Norman Conquest, and in parts much longer. A Victorian history professor at Oxford, when asked by an American visitor to be taken to Oxford's most ancient monument, is said to have taken him outside the town centre to the grassy expanse of Port Meadow. Like at Farmoor, the Thames Valley inhabitants had been grazing their animals on this meadow since prehistory.

Farmoor and Port Meadow fall within a very prominent zone of Darby's map of Domesday meadow. Measured either in acres or in the numbers of plough-teams that may be grazed upon them, it would appear that the richest belt of meadowland coincides neatly with the vales formed over the Jurassic and Cretaceous clay belts lying to the north of the chalk escarpment. These vales are drained by the Upper Thames Valley in the west, and the Great Ouse in the east. As we have seen in Chapter 7, the Upper Thames floodplain has contained large stretches of open grassland since at least the second millennium BC, and the valley has been densely settled within a very open landscape since at least the first millennium, a period during which the Great Ouse also became heavily settled.

The Domesday Book makes a clear distinction between *prata*, or meadow, and *pascua*, or pasture. Meadow was grassland that bordered a river or stream, was liable to floods, and was cut for hay, and pasture was land that was available all year round for the grazing of cattle and sheep. We are still uncertain when the cutting of hay first became a regular practice. It was clearly established by the period of Roman rule, as the hay cutting scythes at Farmoor and elsewhere demonstrate.

As yet the botanical evidence from prehistory generally reflects grasslands that were constantly grazed, and which should therefore be described as pasture. Nevertheless the animals that grazed on the floodplain in the summer must have eaten something during the winter months; perhaps the need for hay meadows was only pressing once the other sources of fodder in the landscape, pasture and woodland, were sufficiently depleted. We can now turn to what the Domesday book has to say about these alternative sources of animal food.

Pasture and woodland

Pasture is one of those categories that King William's commissioners often glossed over as being of marginal interest in terms of the survey's main purpose. It is rarely mentioned for the north of England, described merely as 'pasture for the cattle of the village' in Cambridgeshire, Hertfordshire and Middlesex, and irregularly recorded elsewhere. We simply get a general impression of expanses of open pasture on the high ground between the valleys, and along the lower ground on the coast. The term pasture clearly covered a wide range of ecosystems, from the bleak expanse that much of Dartmoor had become, the lush grasslands that had developed on the chalk hills, to the coastal marshes given over to the grazing of sheep in Essex.

The commissioners paid more attention to the recording of woods, and, like meadow and pasture, the use that is regularly cited is the feeding of animals, in this case pigs. Indeed in much of the south and east, the extent of the woods is actually assessed in terms of the number of pigs it will support. In Lincolnshire, reference is frequently made to *Silua pastilis*, or wood pasture, indicating that other farm animals were grazed in certain woodlands. *Silua pastilis* is distinguished from *Silua minuta*, or coppice woodland, reminding us of the vital function of woods as sources of fuel and building materials.

Oliver Rackham has argued that the majority of the woodlands recorded in the survey broadly correspond in nature, and almost in extent, to the managed woodlands that survived around many villages into the earlier twentieth century. They had been in heavy use, as we saw in Chapter 8, for thousands of years prior to the Norman period, and they continued in heavy use until recently superseded by commercial forestry.

In addition to the vills that had their own heavily managed woodlands, there were an equal number that did not. In some counties, woodland made up less than five per cent of the land surface, reflecting the extent of progressive clearance over the preceding millennia. In a few places, much larger tracts survived, allocated to and used by a number of vills, and covering tens of thousands of hectares. In addition to the Weald itself, there was a massive wood spreading from the Buckinghamshire Chilterns through to Essex, the woods later to be named 'Arden' in Warwickshire, and 'Lyme' in Cheshire, and two further stretches in Staffordshire and Derbyshire. I have hesitated to call these 'forests', as this term has changed its meaning a number of times in history, and in the eleventh century had a quite distinct meaning from 'woodland'. It may be more useful to examine the Norman term 'forest' together with another rather ambiguous category, 'waste'.

Forests and waste

The original meaning of 'forest' was 'outside', and was used in the eleventh century to denote land that the king had placed outside common law. The reason he did so was to release tracts of land in order that he and his fellow Norman lords could persue their passionate love of hunting within them. These forests were often wooded, but could encompass a variety of ecosystems; in some forests there might hardly be a tree in sight. The word referred to a legal, and not an ecological, unit of land.

In a similar way, the meaning of 'waste' in the Domesday Book is not heathland or moorland. These, as we have seen, were either ignored by the commissioners, and show up on Darby's maps as areas of very low population, or were included in the pasture component of the settlements on their fringes. The word is instead used to refer to the laying waste of settlements during the various upheavals of the eleventh century, and particularly the 'harrying of the north' with which King William concluded his conquest of the land. The commissioners quite probably used the term to describe any derelict settlement they found reverting to scrub, whatever the reasons for its abandonment.

So while the previous categories related to the workings of a thriving medieval settlement within its farmlands and near to its managed woodland, forest and waste both refer to land that had been taken out of that economic system, usually by the king. In some cases the two terms are very closely linked. The Domesday Book's account of the sites of eleven settlements that lay waste on the Hereford-Radnor border, 'On these waste lands woods have grown up which the said Osbern has the hunting and takes what he can get. Nothing else.', graphically illustrates how land waste could easily become forest. King William is said to have lain waste several settlements in order to create the New Forest in Hampshire.

The New Forest is one of the few forests that receives extended mention in the survey; they were clearly not regarded as central to its brief, and only 25 receive passing reference. However, the 1087 entry in the Anglo-Saxon Chronicle refers to the large forests of deer created by the new king. By the twelfth century his successors had put up to a third of England outside common law in this way.

The survey is far more explicit on the extent of settlement that had been laid waste. The record for the north is littered with the words *Wasta est*, especially in Yorkshire, where William is said to have 'laid waste all the shire'. The northern survey provides some depressing hints at poverty, ruin and abandonment. Earl Tosti's manor of Preston, for example, is recorded as containing 61 villages. In 1086, amongst all these villages in the manor, only 6.5 ha (16 acres) were still being cultivated, it was not known exactly by whom. Of the remainder the survey has no more to say than '*Reliqua sunt wasta*'.

CONSTANT RECOVERY AND THE MODERN LEGACY

This sad episode that ends our account of the development of the human landscape was nevertheless no more final than any of the earlier episodes we have examined in this book. As we saw in the second chapter, the ecosystem is a dynamic entity that does not linger in any modified state. Just as the wildwood of prehistory quickly returned after disturbance to some more stable state, so a wasted vill would either tumble down to woodland or return to cultivation within a relatively short period.

The Domesday returns for Cheshire provide numbers of wasted vills in that county at three stages between 1066 and 1086. By this latter date, 104 of the 162 wasted vills of 15 years earlier had already regained some semblance of normality; the landscape was on its way to recovery, but not without scars to join the scars and hallmarks of previous millennia of human occupation.

In the first chapter of this book, reference was made to the contribution of the geographer, W. G. Hoskins, who drew our attention to the historic nature of the English landscape. He managed to demonstrate how those 'scars and hallmarks' of past human activity within the environment have continually remoulded its form, such that we can perceive in the modern landscape a whole series of earlier epochs of human ecology.

When Hoskins wrote *The Making of the English Landscape* in 1955, the patterns were clearest for the periods that followed the writing of the Domesday Book. The structure of villages and towns, and the major lines of communication, could be related in turn to medieval settlement, medieval and parliamentary enclosure, and the Industrial Revolution.

In the 30 years that have elapsed since that impressive contribution was made, our knowledge has grown considerably. We can now more fully appreciate the patterns that relate to the emergence, as well as to the subsequent development, of the Domesday landscape. In among the medieval and enclosure fields we can detect boundaries that belong to prehistory. Beyond these fields lie vast areas of heathland, itself an artifice of early farming. The wildwood it replaced may have gone, but back in the valleys the surviving patches of coppiced woodland are its direct descendants.

We have seen how each one of these landscapes also preserves a wealth of evidence of how they came into being, and how, when subjected to the techniques of landscape archaeology and environmental archaeology, they can be made to yield a record of England before Domesday. Those techniques are still young and growing fast; the record will no doubt develop and change as all such records should. In the meantime I hope this book has provided a glimpse of the fruitful and stimulating nature of these studies, and of the contribution they have already made to an appreciation of our dynamic and ever-changing landscape.

Further reading

Chapter One: Back beyond history (pp. 7–24)

M. L. Shackley (1981) *Using environmental archaeology* London, Batsford

J. G. Evans (1978) *Introduction to environmental archaeology* London, Paul Elek

I. G. Simmons & M. J. Tooley, eds. (1981) *The environment in British prehistory* London, Duckworth

L. V. Grinsell & P. J. Fowler (1972) *Archaeology and the landscape* London, Baker

P. J. Fowler, ed. (1975) *Recent work in rural archaeology* Bradford-on-Avon, Moonraker Press

P. J. Fowler & J. G. Evans (1967) Ploughmarks, lynchets and early fields. *Antiquity* 41 289–291

J. M. Steane & B. F. Dix (1978) *Peopling Past Landscapes* London, Council for British Archaeology

D. Walker (1965) The post-glacial period in the Langdale Fells, English Lake District. *New Phytologist* 64 488–510

M. Aston & T. Rowley (1974) *Landscape archaeology: an introduction to fieldwork techniques on post-Roman landscapes* Newton Abbot, David & Charles

M. Aston (1985) *Interpreting the landscape: landscape archaeology in local studies* London, Batsford

Chapter Two: Searching for a wildscape (pp. 25–39)

G. W. Dimbleby (1977) *Ecology and archaeology* London, Edward Arnold

W. Pennington (1974) *The history of British vegetation* London, English Universities Press

H. Godwin (1975) *The history of the British Flora* Cambridge University Press

E. P. Odum (1975) *Ecology* New York, Holt

P. A. Colinvaux (1973) *Introduction to ecology* New York, Wiley

Chapter Three: Breaking ground and tipping the balance (pp. 40–52)

P. Mellars (1978) *The early postglacial settlement of northern Europe* London, Duckworth

T. Ingold (1980) *Hunters, pastoralists and ranchers* Cambridge University Press

J. G. D. Clark (1954) *Star Carr* Cambridge University Press

B. Bender (1975) *Farming in prehistory: from hunter-gatherer to food producer* London, Baker

G. Barker (1985) *Prehistoric farming in Europe* Cambridge University Press

R. Dennell (1983) *European economic prehistory: a new approach* London, Academic Press

S. Cole (1970) *The Neolithic Revolution* London, British Museum

P. J. Fowler (1983) *The farming of prehistoric Britain* Cambridge University Press

P. J. Ucko & G. W. Dimbleby (1969) *The domestication and exploitation of plants and animals* London, Duckworth

Chapter Four: A landscape of ancestors (pp. 53–69)

C. Burgess (1980) *The age of Stonehenge* London, Dent

P. Ashbee *et al.* (1979) Excavations of three long barrows near Avebury, Wiltshire *Proceedings of the Prehistoric Society* 45

R. W. Smith (1984) The ecology of Neolithic farming systems as exemplified by the

Avebury region of Wiltshire *Proceedings of the Prehistoric Society* 50
R. Mercer (1980) *Hambledon Hill: a neolithic landscape* Edinburgh University Press
J. G. Evans (1972) *Land snails in archaeology* London, Seminar Press
Royal Commission on Historical Monuments (England) (1979) *Stonehenge and its environs* Edinburgh University Press

Chapter Five: Field-boundaries and frontiers (pp. 70–89)
H. C. Bowen & P. J. Fowler (1978) *Early land allotment* Oxford, British Archaeological Reports
C. C. Taylor (1975) *Fields in the English landscape* London, J. M. Dent
D. Riley (1980) *Early landscapes from the air* Sheffield University, Department of Archaeology
A. Fleming (1978, 1983) The prehistoric landscape of Dartmoor *Proceedings of the Prehistoric Society* 44 & 49
K. Smith *et al.* (1981) The Shaugh Moor Project *Proceedings of the Prehistoric Society* 47
N. D. Baalam *et al.* (1982) The Shaugh Moor Project *Proceedings of the Prehistoric Society* 48
J. C. Richards (1978) *The archaeology of the Berkshire Downs* Reading, Berkshire Archaeology Unit
R. Bradley & A. Ellison (1975) *Ram's Hill* Oxford, British Archaeological Reports

Chapter Six: Gathering together (pp. 90–105)
B. W. Cunliffe (1983) *Danebury: anatomy of an Iron Age Hill Fort* London, Batsford
B. W. Cunliffe (1978) *Iron Age communities in Britain* London, Routledge and Kegan Paul
J. Wacher (1978) *Towns of Roman Britain* London, Batsford
A. R. Hall & H. K. Kenward (1982) *Environmental archaeology in the urban context* London, Council for British Archaeology
A. R. Hall *et al.* (1980) Environmental evidence from Roman deposits at Skeldergate. *The archaeology of York* 14/3 London, Council for British Archaeology

A. R. Hall *et al* (1983) Environment and living conditions at two Anglo-Scandinavian sites. *The archaeology of York* 14/4 London, Council for British Archaeology
H. K. Kenward & D. Williams (1979) Biological evidence from the Roman warehouses in Coney Street *The archaeology of York* 14/2 London, Council for British Archaeology

Chapter Seven: Smallholdings and survival (pp. 106–21)
P. J. Reynolds (1979) *Iron-Age Farm: the Butser experiment* London, Colonnade
B. W. Cunliffe (1978) *Iron Age communities in Britain* London, Routledge and Kegan Paul
P. J. Fowler (1983) *Farms in England: prehistoric to present* London, Royal Commission for Historic Monuments
B. W. Cunliffe & D. Miles, eds. (1984) *Aspects of the Iron Age in central southern Britain* Oxford, Committee for Archaeology
M. Parrington (1978) *Excavations of an Iron Age settlement, Bronze Age ring ditches and Roman features at Ashville Trading Estate, Abingdon, Oxfordshire* London, Council for British Archaeology
G. Lambrick & M. Robinson (1979) *Iron Age and Roman riverside settlements at Farmoor, Oxfordshire* London, Council for British Archaeology
P. J. Fasham (1985) *Winnall Down* Hampshire Field Club
Cleveland County Archaeological Unit (1985) *Recent excavations in Cleveland*
D. Knight (1984) *Late Bronze Age and Iron Age settlement in the Nene and Great Ouse basins* Oxford, British Archaeological Reports
J. C. Chapman & H. C. Mytum, eds. (1983) *Settlement in Northern Britain 1000 BC to AD 1000* Oxford, British Archaeological Reports
C. C. Taylor (1984) *Village and farmstead*

Chapter Eight: The last of the wildwood (pp. 122–35)
O. Rackham (1976) *Trees and woodland in the British landscape* London, Dent

O. Rackham (1980) *Ancient woodland* London, Edward Arnold

M. Bell & S. Limbrey, eds. (1982) *Archaeological aspects of woodland ecology* Oxford, British Archaeological Reports

Somerset Levels Papers Vol. 1–, 1975 onwards

J. M. Coles & B. Orme (1982) *Prehistory of the Somerset Levels* Hertford, Stephen Austin & Sons

B. & J. M. Coles (1986) *Sweet Track to Glastonbury* London, Thames & Hudson

Chapter Nine: The blasted heath (pp. 136–47)

J. G. Evans *et al.* (1975) *The effect of man on the landscape: the highland zone* London, Council for British Archaeology

S. Limbrey *et al.* (1978) *The effect of man on the landscape: the lowland zone* London, Council for British Archaeology

S. Limbrey (1975) *Soils and archaeology*

M. Bell (1983) Valley sediments as evidence of prehistoric land use on the South Downs *Proceedings of the Prehistoric Society* 49

G. W. Dimbleby (1962) *The development of British heathlands and their soils* Oxford Forestry Memoirs

Chapter Ten: The emergence of a Domesday landscape (pp. 148–62)

J. G. Hurst (1979) *Wharram Percy: a study of settlement on the Yorkshire Wolds* London, Society for Mediaeval Archaeology

T. Rowley (1978) *Villages in the landscape* London, Dent

T. Rowley, ed. (1981) *The origins of open field agriculture* London, Croom Helm

C. C. Taylor (1974) *Fieldwork in medieval archaeology* London, Batsford

P. H. Sawyer, ed. (1976) *Medieval settlement: continuity and change* London, Edward Arnold

J. M. Steane (1985) *The archaeology of mediaeval England and Wales* London, Croom Helm

M. Gelling (1978) *Signposts to the past: placenames and the history of England* London, Dent

M. L. Faull, ed. (1984) *Studies in late Anglo-Saxon settlement* Oxford University Department for External Studies

General Index

Index of sites and localities